FRANCE
ACTUALLY

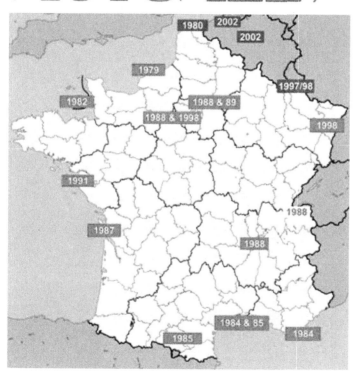

North / South Divide – Volume 4

Interesting Books...
...Fascinating Subjects!

Publishing

www.poshupnorth.com

This edition published in Great Britain in March 2022 by
Posh Up North Publishing, Beckenham Road, Wallasey, United Kingdom

ISBN-13: 978-1-909643-47-5

LIST OF CONTENTS

INTRODUCTION

This book has not been written as a serious commercial venture. By that, I mean that I don't expect millions of people all over the world to want to buy it and I am not expecting to make any money out of selling it. But it is, at least, available should somebody somewhere feel that need...

I had a bout of ill health in 2020 and, had things worked out differently, I might not have been here now to write these lines.

Luckily I am - more or less - back to normal now – but the whole experience made me reflect upon the fact that, if anything HAD happened to me, then the whole melange of memories, experiences, interesting stories and other trivia that has been accumulated in my brain over 50 or so years would all be lost.

I thought that would be a bit of a shame so, as a sort of "self healing therapy", I decided to write the more interesting things down for the benefit of future generations.

This book is mainly aimed at friends and family members – ie: people who know me and may remember some of the episodes that I have recounted - and I hope they might find the stories interesting and enjoyable.

If, however, you haven't a clue who I am and still want to read this book, then I hope there is enough general interest information for you to be able to enjoy it as well.

Paul Breeze
Wallasey, March 2022

Cover Photos
Front Cover: Map of France showing the dates of Paul's various visits
Back Cover: Paul in Paris in 1988, with the Eiffel Tower in the background

A Note On Photos:

A lot of the photos in this book are a bit ropey, for which I apologise - but there is not much I can do about it.

As we are looking back at things that happened 30 or 40 years ago in some cases, they are all scanned from old photographic prints and many of those originals are not very good either.

You can take a much better image on your phone these days than was possible with the average amateur family camera back in the old days and you can immediately check whether the shot actually has come out rather than having to wait to finish the film and then send it away to be developed.

The problem with making a high quality digital scan of a poor original image is that it tends to enhance the impurities as well as the basic picture – and there are complicated technical things like colour separations to think about as well.

So, some photos are better than others but they are the only ones I have got and I hope they will serve to illustrate the stories included in this book.

Technical Disclaimer – Please Read!

I am not a qualified engineer nor am I a trained printer. The descriptions of the workings of the printing presses that I have included in this book are for illustrative purposes only and are based purely on my own observations, rather than any particular technical expertise or training.

If you are planning on operating or adjusting a printing press, please make sure that you are fully trained by a qualified person before doing so and that all operating instructions and safety procedures are correctly followed.

My grandad – an excellent engineer – doing what I, apparently, also do best, ie "supervising", at the Alley Trailers factory in Burnham Market, early 1950s. (PR Photo)

1950s: Early Family Voyages

From Rhodesia to Ramsey!

I have always been fascinated by the concept of "abroad", and was actually almost born abroad – twice in fact!

The first time that I was almost born abroad (now, this might sound a bit weird but please bear with me – it all makes perfect sense to me ...) was in the mid 1950s when my mum's family were planning on emigrating to Rhodesia – which is now known as Zimbabwe, but back then was a thriving British colony.

Her dad – my grandad – Francis James Whittington (1908-1992), who was known to everybody as "Jim", was the engineering manager for the Alley brothers agricultural equipment designers and manufacturers, which was based in Burnham Market in Norfolk.

He had originally worked as a troubleshooter for the Caterpillar Tractor Company and, in the 1930s, had been head hunted to maintain the Alleys' farm machinery at Blue Stone Farm in South Creake in Norfolk, which was the first fully mechanised farm in the country.

The Alleys went on to found Farmers' Glory cornflakes – as a domestic equivalent to the popular USA invented Kellogs – and had a factory in Godmanchester, near Huntingdon, where my grandad also had a leading role - and my mum was born while they were living there.

Anyway, by the 1950s, they were designing and manufacturing bespoke farming machinery for the agricultural industry and my grandad was in charge of all the workshops.

At some point Eric Alley decided to close the Burnham Market factory and move the whole enterprise to Rhodesia – which used to be known as the "Bread Basket of Africa" and had a good reputation for exporting wheat, tobacco and corn to other African countries and elsewhere around the world.

My grandad and family were planning to go with him but then my mum's mum's mum – my mum's grandmother, my great grandmother – was taken ill and her mum (my grandmother) didn't want to leave until she had fully recovered. So everything was put back.

Then my mum's vaccinations for travelling abroad didn't take and the travel plans were once again thrown into disarray.

At that point, according to the family story, my granddad who I, apparently, take after in getting fed up with things easily, decided that it was not worth all the hassle and that they wouldn't go after all. They had given up their house in Norfolk by that time and also disposed of all their furniture ready to start again in Rhodesia so were a bit stuck. They ended up moving to Ramsey where my grandmother's parents were by then living.

I have never been able to establish why my maternal grandparents had moved to Ramsey and nobody else had been able to tell me either, so that is a bit of a mystery - but as it is where my mum went on to meet my dad, I am, obviously, very pleased that they did...

So that is the story of how I might otherwise have been born in Rhodesia, although with all the turmoil that the unfortunate country has been beset with over the intervening decades – not to mention the more recent trend for evicting white farmers off their own land and murdering them – in retrospect, I suppose I was jolly lucky that I wasn't ...!

Emigrating to other British colonies was a very big thing in the 1950s as people wanted to escape the drabness and rationing of post WW2 Britain.

In fact, unlike now where they do their best to find reasons to keep people out, the Australian Government introduced the Assisted Passage Migration Scheme which offered subsidised travel (the famous "Ten Pound Poms") and streamlined settlement procedures to try and attract people to come and populate the country and man its rapidly growing industries.

My grandad's younger brother Syd (1916 -) took his family to Australia and, with him having 8 children and most of those having lots of children and grandchildren, there is now a huge clan of Whittington descendents living in Tasmania and elsewhere down under.

Their sister middle Ruby (1910 -) married somebody called Sharpe and they and their two sons went to live in South Africa.

My grandparents Jim and Nellie Whittington at Bluestone Farm, Norfolk, in the 1930s. The chap on the right is possibly Stephen Alley.

My mum and dad (far right of photo) – 1950s at Abbey Flats, Ramsey. This is the only photo that exists of my dad wearing a dinner jacket! Also in the photo are (from left to right) my grandparents – Nellie and Jim Whittington, Len and Nancy Isley (grandmother's younger sister), Jack and Ivy Bayly (her older sister).

The SS Empress Of France (from a Postcard by CR Hoffman, Southampton)

Saskatchewan, Canada

The second time that I was almost born abroad came in the late 1950s when I was almost born in Canada.

Shorty after he had married my mum, my dad travelled to Canada with a view to taking over a farm that his uncle had over there.

I am told he was an "uncle" but haven't been able to establish this for a fact as part of my ongoing family tree research. His name was George Gray - and that fits in because my dad's grandmother on that side was called Elizabeth Gray (1870-1957) and she originally came from Sheffield.

Unfortunately, there are numerous Elizabeth Grays and George Grays in Sheffield on the various censuses covering that period and without any other reference points, it is impossible to work out which they may be. So I know very little about George Gray other than he existed and he had a farm in Saskatchewan, Canada.

We do have this photo of him driving a hay cart, although it's not so clear that you could recognise him if you saw him in the street, and there is also an aerial photo of the farm, which also doesn't help to identify it as I am sure there must be thousands of farms that look exactly the same across the North American continent.

I can only assume – although we don't know this either – that George didn't have any sons of his own otherwise they would have presumably taken over the running of the farm themselves...

The original plan had been that my dad's younger brother Brian (1936-1972) would go and work with George Gray and eventually take over the farm. Records show that Brian sailed for Halifax Nova Scotia on the Cunard White Star liner RMS Samaria on the 16th January 1952.

He travelled on his own and was only 15 at the time, which might sound a bit daunting, but you have to remember that, back then, people routinely left school at 14 and went out to work – and were generally less pampered and protected than youngsters are today.

When I was little, I remember that we had some photos of Brian working on the farm in Canada – possibly taken at the same time as the George Gray photo - but they seem to have got lost over the years. This is a shame as they are the only photos we ever had of him.

For some reason, Brian's plans for Canada didn't work out so it was then decided that my dad might go over there and take over the farm instead.

He had already been abroad when he went to Hamburg during his National Service with the army – and always impressed me when I was little that he knew how to say "Wie spät is es?" and "Zwei Bier, bitte" in German...

My dad was also due to go to the Korean War but, as his National Service period was due to finish before he would have arrived there, he was told that he didn't have to go.   So, stretching my earlier points somewhat, had things turned out differently, I might also have been born in Germany or Korea as well...

So, my dad – Roy Edward Breeze (1932-1995), who for some reason was registered as Edward Roy on his birth certificate (possibly kingly pretentions on the part of his parents...?) but was always known to all his friends as "Jo", sailed from Liverpool on the Canadian Pacific Railway Company's RMS Empress Of France on 6th June 1958 bound for Montreal.

From Montreal. he took a train to his destination in Saskatchewan. We don't actually know where the farm was, unfortunately, so that leaves a big hole in this story but - just as a guide - the rail journey from Montreal to Saskatoon, which is pretty much in the middle of the Province, is 2500 Km long and these days takes around 60 hours - or the best part of 3 days.

Making allowances for less efficient rolling stock, and more stops at little stations along the way, you can imagine that it would have been quite a journey in the 1950s...

As it turned out, my dad didn't have to make the whole journey to Saskatchewan on the train as there was a dramatic occurrence.

The train was stopped en route and a Royal Canadian Mounted Policeman – in full "Mountie" apparel – came on to find my dad. He was told that his uncle had committed suicide and he was taken off the train and driven (probably not on horseback....) to wherever it was that they needed to go.

This scuppered any chance my dad might have had of learning the ropes and taking over the farm but he had to hang round until things were sorted out.

In fact, as he hadn't planned on coming back to England – my mum was going to travel over and join him once things were settled - my dad didn't have a return ticket and had no money to come back anyway.

He ended up having to stay in Canada for 6 months until HIS dad was able to save enough money to pay for his return voyage.

After all that excitement, my Mum and Dad settled in Peterborough and I came along a few years later...

Above left: My mum and dad - Joy and Roy – pre-me, at Woodhurst Road in Stanground, early 1960s. Above right: Me with my dad at Clacton in 1968.

Above left: Not sure where this is – possibly Gorleston or Gt Yarmouth – but it must be 1970 or 71 as the slot machines are pre-decimal currency. Above middle: Family at Hunstanton. This must 1972 as my little brother Gary is the pram. Above right: 1976 at Brancaster beach on a visit to Auntie Doris and Uncle Reg

1979 on the beach while at Butlins in Skegness

14

Staycating

After all that globetrotting and "almost" globetrotting, nobody in my immediate family actually went abroad again until 1979 when I went on a school trip to France.

I knew of friends at school who went on package holidays to Majorca or wherever but that was still fairly rare when I was little and most people used to go on holiday to places in this country.

My dad worked as a lorry driver and was out all day all week so, I suppose, he liked to relax at home when he could – and the idea of travelling somewhere for a "break" would not have appealed to him as much as it might to somebody who was office-bound for a living.

I know that we went on a holiday to Clacton when I was very little – as I have seen photos from it, although I was too small to actually remember it.

I do remember a holiday in Gorleston on the Norfolk coast near to Great Yarmouth and, once my younger brother came along, we went on a couple of caravan holidays to Hunstanton which, despite only being about 50 miles from Peterborough - and the sort of place where people now pop for a day out, back then it took ages to get to as the roads (and the cars) were not nearly so good and a trip there was quite an undertaking.

One place that we did use to go to regularly - once a year, anyway - was to visit Auntie Doris and Uncle Reg in Burnham Thorpe.

They weren't proper blood relations but had been my granny and grandad's next door neighbours when they had lived in that area when my mum was growing up. They had a daughter called Jean who was a similar age to my mum and Uncle Reg had worked at the Alley factory with grandad so they all spent a lot of time together. My mum always referred to them as "Auntie" and "Uncle", so we did as well.

After my mum and grandparents had moved away, they kept in touch and went to see them regularly and after my grandparents had retired, they often went to stay for a week.

When I used to go, the area was beautiful, tranquil and untouched. I understand that, after the property boom of the late 1980s, lots of stockbroker types from London bought up all the rural properties around there and turned them into weekend homes, thus ruining the traditional village life.

Certainly the last time I was there, Burnham Overy Staithe - which used to be nice for exploring the sand dunes, walking on the beach and strolling along the peaceful water front was over-run with uncouth yuppies with boats and Range Rovers...

The main market town is Burnham Market – and that's where the trains used to go to until 1952 when the passenger service was discontinued and 1964 when the freight service stopped as well

Then there are all the villages around it – in no particular order: Burnham Thorpe – where I used to go to, Burnham Deepdale, Burham Norton, Burnham Sutton and Burnham Westgate.

As I mentioned earlier, Burnham Overy is on the coast and has nice beach access and we often used to go to nearby Brancaster which was a bit more commercialised. Then there were the towns of Wells-next-the-Sea and Sheringham a bit further along the coast.

One year – I'm sure it was 1976 because I remember the Montreal Olympic games being on the television – it was arranged for me to go and stay with Auntie Doris and Uncle Reg for a week.

It turned out – although I didn't know this at the time (people didn't "inform" kids about things back then like they do now – you just got presented things as a fait accompli and did them...) that my granny had already been staying there and was ready to come home.

If I remember this rightly, granddad wasn't staying there and he went to bring her back and I went with him with my suitcase.

He then stayed for lunch and went back home to Ramsey with granny during the afternoon, leaving me there for the week.

I seem to think that, at the end of my week's stay, mum and dad and Gary came for their annual visit and took me back with them.

Quite how all that was arranged without the benefit of modern inventions like Facebook, emails and mobile phones, I couldn't tell you – but things still used to get done!

I don't really remember what I did when during that visit. I remember that the weather was mostly nice although it did rain on the day we went "fun shopping" in Burnham Market.

Uncle Reg had a new box kite that he was experimenting with and we went up on top of a hill to try that out.

Auntie Doris used to help out at the local church and had a regular day when she went in to clean. Burnham Thorpe was the birthplace of naval hero Lord Horatio Nelson and, as his father had been the rector, he is greatly celebrated in the church. She took me one day to have a look round and there were naval flags hanging from the ceiling – it all looked very impressive.

A Wet Week In Hunstanton...

While we are on the subject of Norfolk... We spent a week in a holiday flat in Hunstanton in the summer of 1977.

We went with Auntie Margaret and Uncle Jim who, like Doris & Reg, were not actual aunts at all but friends of my mum and dad who they had met on holiday a long time ago and kept in touch with over the years.

They had actually emigrated to Canada for a while but later came back to England and lived not far from us in Stanground with their daughter Janie.

You might recall that the summer of 1976 was hot and sunny for a long period of time and there were water shortages. Well, 1977 made up for it as it rained all summer.

Aside from the fact that it rained nearly the whole time we were there, the only other reason that I remember that I can identify that this was 1977 was because we had Top of The Pops on the TV one evening before going out for a bracing "sod it - we ARE on holiday" walk along the sea front and it had Barry Biggs singing "Life Is A Three Ring Circus" on it - and that was in the charts in August 1977. So there you are - good old YouTube...

Don't ask me what else we did for the week. Got cold and wet mostly, I seem to remember....

Cub Camp

Paul as a Cub Scout, 1976

On another occasion - and I can't remember whether this was 1976 or 1977 – I went camping with my cub scout pack – the Peterborough 39th St John's.

I'm not sure where we went but it can't have been very far out of Peterborough as we just went in cars and it didn't take very long.

It must have been at some outdoor pursuits centre of some sort because it wasn't a wild camping expedition in the middle of nowhere. The main building had a large dining area, kitchen, toilets and showers and also dormitories for anybody who didn't want to sleep outside in the tent.

Having signed up to go camping, I was determined to sleep under canvas and we had even borrowed a sleeping bag off our next door neighbours (who were keen campers and, later, caravanners) for the weekend.

Here again, I don't really remember what we did on this trip. We certainly didn't do any of the typical scouty things like knots or tracking but I do have a vague recollection of cooking some sausages at one point over a top heavy and unsafe looking Calor gas stove in the middle of a field.

I think we played a lot of football – and I distinctly remember one of the scout leaders was sitting in his car listening to the radio and calling out the Peterborough United latest scores when they announced.

One aspect of the camp that I do remember was that we had a campfire evening where we all sat round listening to stories and singing songs. There were funny recitations like "We're Going On A Lion Hunt" and also a group rendition of the popular scout song "Ging Gang Goolie", which I didn't know all the words to.

19

This is about the only photo from the trip to the Forest of Dean that comes out anywhere near clear enough to do anything with. Here you can see our teacher Mr Richard Perkins (on the left) and two other people doing something really interesting - but I couldn't say what. In the background is the mess tent where we used to eat – and the ship's bell that announced mealtimes.

1978: Forest of Dean

In July 1978, I went camping again but this time with my school – Southfield Junior School - to the Forest of Dean. It's quite a way to the Forest of Dean from Peterborough even now and with a coach - on the old roads - and kids wanting toilet stops every so often, it would have taken even longer back then, so this really was quite an adventure.

It was just a group of us 4th years who went on this trip and the numbers were made up with kids from two other schools – Houghton near St Ives (that's the St Ives in Cambridgeshire not the one in Cornwall) and another one that I don't remember the name of – and they travelled separately so we met them when we arrived at the campsite.

We were all mixed up into groups of 6 or 8 to share a tent, with boys and girls strictly segregated of course...

As far as I can recall, apart from a couple of days, the weather was gloriously sunny and we did lots of walking in the countryside.

We saw the stunning views from Symonds Yat Rock and crossed the River Wyre on a not very study looking wire bridge - and one day we went out "orienteering" where we were sent off in groups armed with a map and compass with instructions to find our own way back to camp.

One memorable excursion that we had was walking across the Severn Bridge. We were dropped off by the coach at one end then and picked up again at the other. The length is apparently 1 mile or so and the bridge is 160m above the river so the views are really worth seeing.

It was a nice bright sunny day when we went but the wind whipping across the bridge was quite breathtaking even then and I certainly wouldn't have wanted to do that in a storm!

After that, we had a shopping trip to Monmouth – across the Welsh border, so that was the first time I had ever left England – even if it wasn't strictly abroad !

On another occasion we went to a Forestry Centre where we were shown how trees are felled safely and saw one being cut up for transportation to the saw mill - and another time we went to a nearby Falconry Centre to see birds of prey being trained.

We also had an excursion to Berkeley Castle – where we heard about how King Edward II had a grizzly end on the premises.

All our meals at the camp were served in a big marquee with long rows of tables and there was a big ship's bell hung by the entrance which was rung when it was time to go in.

In the evenings after supper, very much like at the cub camp - we used to sit around in the marquee listening to stories and singing songs – things like "The Quartermaster's Stores", "Bravo, Bravo, Very Well Done" and "Merrily We Roll Along" leap to mind here.

One evening, we had a talent contest where anybody who wanted to could take to the floor and do a turn.

Karl Lillicrap and I did an appallingly high pitched duet rendition of Kate Bush's "Wuthering Heights" which had been a big number one hit earlier in the year – and which everybody thought was great – obviously....

On another evening, after it had got dark, we went "Deer Stalking" in the forest. It was quite exciting at the time but, looking back now with the wiser knowledge of a mature(ish..) adult, quite how likely it was that with 50 or so laughing chattering 11 years olds all brandishing torches and stomping about, we would ever get anywhere near a deer, I can't really imagine...

Above left: Frazer Gray, Mark Fuller and PB larking about at summer Camp, July 1978

Above right: Paul's brother Gary, dad Roy and friend Craig Moran at Expo 78 at the East of England Showground. I met Craig at camp in the Forest of Dean. He lived at RAF Wyton where his dad was in the air force. He went to Houghton School and was billeted in our tent. We met up a few times over the summer.

Above left: Brother Gary and PB on a slide at Butlins, Skegness in July1979.
Above right: Mum (Joy) and brother Gary outside our chalet at Butlins.

1979: Butlins

I am slipping out of chronological order slightly here as these next few entries all refer to staycations as well – or domestic trips, anyway.

"Staycation" – that's wonderful modern word isn't it....?

The term didn't exist until a few years ago and when I was little, they were just called "holidays", irrespective where you went to...

We went on holiday to Butlins at Skegness in Summer 1979.

In fact, the camp is situated in a village called Ingoldmells just outside Skegness and, for once, I can narrow down exactly the dates that we were there as a couple of big media happenings at the time.

I distinctly remember seeing on the TV in our Butlins holiday flat that Sebastian Coe broke the world record for the Dream Mile at the Bislett games in Oslo with a time of 3m48.9 (I just looked that up...) – and, according to the British Newspaper Archive, that was on Tuesday 17th July.

Also MPs in parliament voted against the reintroduction of the death penalty while we were there and I remember seeing the result on the front of some of the news papers in the site shop – and that vote was held on Thursday 19th July (362 against 243 for...)

So I can safely say that we were at Butlins in Skegness for the week of 16th to 20th July 1979 – probably arriving on the Saturday before and leaving on the Saturday after - or whenever their changeover day happened to be back then.

That must have been the first week of the school holidays as it seems quite early to me - but we certainly never went away during school time, unless it was an organised school trip.

Anyway, you know all about Butlins. Wall to wall fun and everything is included in the price. Except that we went self catering, so our meals weren't included. And I seem to think that you had to put coins in a meter to use the electricity in the holiday flats.

And you had to have a huge stack of 50p pieces to be able to make the television work.

But certainly all the entertainment and leisure activities were free – or at least, included in the package price.

They had a very good programme of kids' activities indoor and outdoor depending on the weather – with different things organised for each morning and afternoon. These were run by the Redcoats – so parents could safely leave their offspring in good hands and go off and do whatever they wanted to.

There was a fairground on the site and you could go an all the rides and attractions as often as you wanted.

There was also a site theatre which had a different show on every night and I really enjoyed going to that. One night it was a variety show – then a comedy play – then a mystery play.

There were also posters up around the place announcing that comedian Mike Read (who would later be better known for playing the long suffering Frank in EastEnders...) was doing a comedy show one evening a week in one of the site bars.

Back on those days, everyone my age knew him from being the host of the kids' TV game show Runaround – but his Butlins shows were strictly for adults only, so I, obviously, didn't get to see him...

On some afternoons, they staged wrestling in one of the bars. This was before the licensing laws had been liberalised and bars were not allowed to sell alcohol between 3pm and 6.30pm. So Butlins rather cleverly made use of one of their venues, which would otherwise have been shut at that time, installed a wrestling ring and had several bouts of wrestling on those afternoons.

Wrestling used to be hugely popular among the Great British public in the 1970s and early 80s – and by this, I mean before the advent of all the over the top American WWF things with snakes and coffins and other silliness.

It used to be a main feature of ITV's World of Sport every Saturday afternoon before the football results came on and they used to show bouts from various venues around the country.

Many of the wrestlers like Big Daddy, Giant Haystacks and Mick McManus were household names at the time and the shows used to especially appeal to old ladies (for some reason...) and kids – so it was an ideal entertainment to put on at Butlin's holiday camps. My guess is that they made a fortune selling tea, coffee and soft drinks and crisps to the spectators - and it was a good way of spending an afternoon – especially if the weather was bad.

Ingoldmells has/had its own beach – within an easy walk from the Butlins camp - and we went out and played on the sand there a few times.

Then, one afternoon – I always thought it was Sunday but it might not have been – depending on which day of the week it was that we actually arrived and departed...- I recall that we walked along the beach from Ingoldmells to Skegness and looked around the fair and the town. It was quite a long way and I think we may have taken the bus back.

One of Auntie Sadie's flying visits in the mid 1980s - taken in granny and grandad's back garden at Church Green, Ramsey. Left to right: PB, dad Roy (Jo), mum Joy, grandad Jim, granny Nellie and Auntie Sadie. Photo probably taken by Gary as he is not in the picture!

1981: Visit To Auntie Sadie's

I wasn't quite sure what year this was – but having checked on the back of one the photographs, luckily my mum always wrote on the back who, what and when (as opposed to previous generations who didn't and have left us with boxes and boxes of old photos and not the slightest clue of who is in any of them ...!) - I can confidently confirm that it was 1981 – August to be precise.

Auntie Sadie (1913-2006), for change, was a real Aunt. In fact, she was my grandad's youngest sister so she was my mum's aunt and my great aunt, and we – that's my mum, dad, Gary and me - all went to visit Auntie Sadie in Suffolk for a week.

She had been very good at running when she was little – apparently she always had to rush to keep up with my granddad, who was 5 years older than her, when he used to walk with her to school and so on - and one year when she was bit older, she won a camera as a prize in a running race.

As a result, Auntie Sadie had the most wonderful collection of Whittington family photos from the old days featuring all the Kent clan – and lots of other people, obviously.

When she was younger, Sadie actually worked for Dennis Thatcher's chemical company and her best friend was Dennis's personal secretary. She had photos of the annual company outings to the seaside and there were some great pictures of a "pre-Maggie" Dennis!

Luckily, on a later visit, she kindly allowed me to take copies of some of the photos so I have a record of what the family members all looked like. I don't know what happened to her photo albums after she died but I am hoping that cousin Richard (Syd's oldest son) might have salvaged them as they are an important historical and social record of family life in the early 20th century.

Auntie Sadie's husband Frank Wilton had died early and they never had any children. However they had both been very involved with the Boys and Girls Brigades and the church in the past and she was very much a go–getter. She had a car – which was quite unusual for an elderly lady in the days that I am remembering - and was always going off to visit people and do things.

She would sometimes turn up at our house out of blue on the way to or from some exciting adventure, tell us about it over a cup of tea and then rush off again. I always remember her as a bit of a tweedy "Miss Marple" type.

Anyway, it came to pass that in August 1981, she managed to stay in one place long enough to find time for us to go and visit her for a week.

The Belvedere (Kent) Whittingtons

My grandad's parents Emily Whittington, nee Durrant (1874-1945) and John Whittington (1869-1948) – and a family shot of Jim, Ruby, Elsie, Sadie & Syd.

Top Row: Esther Hannah (1894-1993), John Charles (1897-1902) choked to death on a piece of bacon, Francis James (1908 – 1992), Ruby Eugenia (1910-?)

Bottom Row: Elsie Florence (1912-1934) killed in an accident with a horse drawn baker's cart, Sadie Grace (1913-2006), Sydney William (1916-?)

She lived in a village called Weeting, near Brandon in Suffolk. I think if we are being exact, Weeting is actually in Norfolk and Brandon is Suffolk, right on the border – but that's by the by...

Although it wasn't especially far away from Peterborough – about 50 miles or so – it was a bit off the beaten track (sorry, Suffolk...!) and not somewhere that we had ever been before. As such, it was quite an adventure!

My overriding memory of that trip – and we did quite a few interesting things while we were there, which I will tell you about shortly – actually involves a "televisual calamity"!

At the time, our local ITV regional channel Anglia was showing episodes of Space 1999 on a weekday evening around 7.30 (I think it was Thursday in the Sapphire and Steel slot, but could be wrong... back in those days all the ITV regions tended to have different programmes on at different times – in later years, for example, you could watch Blockbusters two or three times in one day by switching between Anglia, Central and Yorkshire, if you happened to be in the right reception area...).

The week before we were due to go to Auntie Sadie's, they showed an episode which - thanks to the modern wonders of Wikipedia - I now know to be called "The Bringers of Wonder".

This is the one where Commander Koenig gets exposed to radiation in an Eagle crash on the moon's surface and, when a rescue ship full of the main cast's relatives suddenly turns up to take the Alphans home, he's the only one who can see that it is an illusion and they are really horrible aliens with an ulterior motive. Appetite whetted? Mine was...

But: it was a two–parter...

And the next episode was due to be screened the week when we were at Auntie Sadie's...

And she didn't own a television!

Now, you couldn't blame her for not having a television, obviously. A lot of older people didn't back then.

They had, after all, been brought up in the days before television had existed and, in a lot of cases, before radio had existed either - so they were used to "making their own entertainment" as it used to be known.

As far as I can ascertain, this used to consist of things like reading, sewing, polishing horse brasses or doing jigsaw puzzles but Auntie Sadie was always off on travels and adventures – or doing church things - or visiting people - so she probably never saw the need.

But for a lad like me brought up in the 1970s, when there were kids' programmes on at tea time – and things like Star Trek and Blake's Seven and the Sweeney in the evenings – and Tiswas and Swap Shop on Saturday morning and stuff like Why Don't You, Champion The Wonder Horse, Robinson Crusoe and a load of bizarre dubbed Czech things on during the holidays, the idea of surviving a whole week without any television was completely unthinkable!

Picture the scene: there's no TV on demand, no catch up (are they the same thing? who knows...), no ITV plus 1, no uploads of old films and TV programmes on YouTube, no DVD box sets – or indeed, DVDs. The majority of normal families didn't even have a VHS video recorder at that time as they were still quite new and very expensive.

So, if you missed a programme when it was on, that was it. You missed it....

Oh – and most televisions didn't have a remote control, so you had to get up from the settee every time you wanted to change channels.

Luckily, you didn't have to do that very often as there were only three of them – BBC1, BBC2 and ITV (Channel 4 didn't start until November 1982).

Anyway, as you will soon discover, we had an enjoyable week at Auntie Sadie's despite her not having any telly.

I seem to think that I read loads of Sven Hassel books - which I insisted on taking as a compromise - and we managed to keep ourselves fully occupied in the pretty Suffolk countryside without even once having to resort to doing jigsaws or polishing horse brasses...

And would you believe that I never did get to see the concluding part of "The Bringers of Wonder" until I was laid up ill during 2020 and discovered that the full set of Space 1999 episodes was available to see on YouTube!

Just across the road from where Auntie Sadie lived was Weeting Castle a medieval manor house built around 1180 by Hugh de Plais, apparently. This was just a ruin having been abandoned in the 14th century – but what a thing to have practically on your doorstep! Needless to say, we had a jolly good look round and thoroughly enjoyed ourselves.

Auntie Sadie also lived within spitting distance (if the wind was in the right direction) of Grimes Graves, the stone age flint mine, so we went there and had a look around the site and the visitor's centre – which was all very interesting. The sort of thing you could tell everybody at school that you had been to, and they would have heard of it and been impressed.

On another occasion we went to visit a nearby stately home that was open to the public and also had very pretty gardens. I always thought it was called Roxburgh Hall but, according to the internet, it can't have been because Roxburgh Hall is in Scotland.

According to mother's useful biro captions on the back of the photos, this was actually called Oxburgh Hall, and a quick look on the internet tells me that it is located halfway between Brandon and Downham Market – so that would be about right.

There was also Brandon Country Park, which I daresay we had a drive round at some point, plus the surrounding Thetford Forest which is a Forestry Commission beauty spot and gives the whole area a completely different feel to the plain flat lands of the Fens around Peterborough.

We also went to see a farm that bred Falabella miniature ponies, which were also very charming.

Photos from top: At Oxburgh Hall with Auntie Sadie, Gary & Dad with the falabella ponies, PB and Gary with pony, Gary at Weeting Castle,
Bottom (left and centre): At Grimes Graves Visitor Centre. (right) PB at Foxhills, Sheringham with tent

32

1983 and after...: Foxhills, Sheringham

In the summer of 1983, my friend John Giddings from Yaxley and I set off on our motorbikes – well, 50cc mopeds, if we are being entirely accurate - for a weekend camping on the north coast of Norfolk.

This was the first time that I had ever gone away completely on my own and under my own steam, so it was quite a special occasion.

I had bought a two man tent from the camping shop in town and we had our sleeping bags and other gear all rolled up tight and packed onto the back of our bikes and off we went.

We had booked onto a campsite called Foxhills – which is near Sheringham and is still, in fact, there today, getting very good reviews on Trip Advisor.

As well as washing facilities etc, the site had a tea room that did decent food so our breakfast and tea was well catered for and we just needed to take a few clothes for the weekend.

Luckily the weather was lovely the whole time we were there so we didn't need very much. The journey was nice along the country roads and with only basic equipment with us, it didn't take long to get set up.

On the Friday evening we went into Sheringham and found a pub that had tables outside and a disco of sorts going on in the yard. We had a non alcoholic drink there – and found somewhere to get some nice seaside fish and chips for supper and went back to the campsite.

Needless to say, once the initial excitement of being in a tent by the seaside had worn off, it was very uncomfortable laying in a sleeping bag on the floor so neither of us slept very well. Plus we kept getting disturbed by noise from other campers in neighbouring tents and caravans – not to mention the odd wildlife sounds that you always hear in the countryside.

The next day – our only full day there - we spent most of time riding along the coast road with its gorgeous views of the sea and exploring all the little villages between Cromer and Weybourne. Then, in the evening, we found somewhere else to go in Sheringham – I think it was village hall or something - that had a disco evening for tourists, and that was about it.

The following day, we packed up our stuff and headed back home.

A few years later, I went back to Foxhills with the same tent but with my girlfriend of the time. I won't mention her name or say anything about her because it would probably all be negative - and, as my mum often says, if you can't say something nice, don't say anything at all.

That particular weekend was marred by the fact the clutch cable broke on her car – but we were lucky enough to find a car mechanic who was holidaying on the site to help us a get new one and fit it for us, so we didn't get stuck.

As time went by - and modes of transport got better – and the roads were vastly improved, it became a lot easier to pop to the Norfolk coast, especially if you were in Peterborough.

I went on numerous occasions, either for the day to Hunstanton or a bit further along the coast, or for a more comfortable weekend in a guest house, but none of these visits stick out in my mind quite as much as the earlier ones that I have described.

The last time that I visited the North Norfolk Coast was when we went to see Lucy's "Auntie" Brenda Rickards – a former neighbour and long term friend of her family - who had retired to live in Holt.

We went to visit her for a few days and this gave me the opportunity to see around some of my old haunts again as we had excursions out to Sheringham, Wells and Cromer.

We even went and saw Auntie Doris on the way home!

Stanground School pupils heading off to France in 1979. Back Row (left to right): John Osbourne, Donna Clark, Derek Runacres, ?, Susan Rowe, ?, Tracey Jepson, Darren McAuley, ?, Michael Haynes, Adrian Wilson, Andrew Chapman, Steven Williamson, Chris Lamb. Front Row: Paul Winskill, Alan Platt, PB, John Giddings, David Nightingale, Stuart Speechley (Photo by Peterborough Evening Telegraph)

1979: Abroad At Last!

I went abroad for the first time in May 1979 on a school trip to Quiberville Sur Mer on the North coast of France.

There was a mix of year groups on the trip. We were the youngest as we were in our first year at Senior School and I think there were some people from the second and third years as well. There may have been some older as well but they wouldn't have had anything to do with us little ones anyway.

I know these year groups are called things like Year 8 and Year 10 these days but at that time, at our school anyway, you entered the first year at age 11 and carried on to the fifth year at age 15. At the end of the fifth year, everybody was 16 and did O Levels and CSEs - as the exams were then - and most people then left school and got a job or an apprenticeship.

It was quite rare for people to stay on in the Sixth Form and do A Levels at that time and for those who did, it was divided into Lower Sixth for the 16 & 17 year olds and Upper Sixth for the 17 to 18 year olds.

We had two coach loads of us going on this trip to France –that's getting on for 100 people - and I don't really remember all the others who went. From the people I knew well, I remember that John Giddings and Mark Eastwood went – and also Alan Platt and Chris Lamb.

We left the school mid afternoon and drove down to Southampton for the overnight ferry crossing to Le Havre. The place we were going to be staying at was actually closer to Dieppe so I don't really know why we took that ferry route – nor why we had to take an overnight crossing – I suppose it was probably cheaper.

My superb memory for trivia reminds me that we sailed outwards on the MV Dragon and back on the MV Leopard. They were both passenger ferries that had been built for Normandy Ferries in the late 1960s. According to simplonpc.co.uk, the two sister ships were both 6100 tons, 416 feet long and could carry 850 passengers and 250 cars.

We travelled on a group passport which was looked after by one of the teachers and I was rather disappointed as I had been looking forward to having my own passport for this trip and getting it stamped like people did on television.

On the ferry we were given reclining seats for the night –which if you have ever tried one are not very relaxing – even less so if you happen to be on a boat full of over-excited kids on school trips.

So, too excited to rest, Gids and I went up on deck to watch the ship draw out of the harbour and went up to the front to feel the rush of sea air on our faces.

I don't remember much else about the channel crossing, other than I hardly slept and probably felt like crap the next morning.

I do remember as we docked at Le Havre getting my first view of French people on French soil and I noticed that the dock workers all wore those blue overalls and had dark caps or berets on - like they always did in films...

The place that we stayed in at Quiberville Sur Mer was called the Colonie de Vacances "Union Lorraine" which - we were never told at the time, but I have since discovered - had originally been built in the 1950s as a holiday destination for children from the steelworking areas of Lorraine where they could go and have some fresh air and a seaside holiday.

We all slept in one long dormitory – there was a separate one for girls, obviously, – and at night a lighthouse from a little way along the coast used to send a beam of light across our windows, making it all seem like a Famous Five adventure.

The centre had a large dining room where we all sat at large tables of 8 or 10 and I remember that we had to take it in turns to clear away and wipe the table down with a cloth after each meal.

I don't actually remember what we had to eat. I imagine that breakfast would have been the typical French holiday fare of bread rolls, nice Normandy butter and those little pots of yogurt they always have.

Often when we went out for the day, we would be given packed lunches to take with us. These invariably consisted of a small sandwich with some ham or salami or some other meat - and occasionally cheese – which nobody that I knew really liked. The thing was that their bread and their meat and their cheese were completely different from what we were used to at home so it was all a bit of a shock.

The irony is that everybody now loves artisanal breads, exotic charcuterie and foreign cheeses – me especially – and I often think that, when I have made myself a sandwich using sourdough bread and parma ham, how similar to those packed lunch sandwiches it actually is!

We were also each given a carton of orange juice with a straw and one of those awful foreign chocolate wafer biscuits that had the wafer on the outside and some sort of powdery chocolate substance in between. If you ever try to eat one of those, the wafer sticks to the roof of your mouth – and, would you believe it, you can get them in Lidl these days. Give me a Penguin any day...!

PB with John Giddings (left) at the Colonie de Vacances "Union Lorraine" at Quiberville sur Mer in 1979. You can clearly see the mer in the background.

Above Left: The view from our dorm window looking out to sea. Above Right: A view of the Colonie de Vacances where we stayed taken from an old postcard from Quiberville sur Mer. Below: The whole postcard.

I do remember that one evening as part of the evening meal, we were given the chance to try some typical French specialities.

Everybody was given a thimbleful of red wine to drink – and a snail in garlicky oil.

We were also given a little piece of chocolate which apparently had ants in – and which I am pleased to say tasted considerably more like chocolate than ants.

While I have had snails on several occasions in France in later years, and frogs legs one time as well - I can't say that I have ever had ants in chocolate again and it doesn't really appeal to me.

Talking of French cuisine – and this is going off the point regarding the trip to Quiberville somewhat but is still vaguely relevant...

While I was in the first year at school – and this would have been earlier in the year than the French trip - as part of our introduction to learning French, we had a "French breakfast" in the small hall.

Our school had two assembly halls – the main hall and the small hall and, as you can probably guess, the small hall was – erm – smaller than the big one.

The main hall had the floor marked out for various indoor sports and they regularly had equipment set up in there for badminton or trampolining. It was also used as the dining room at lunchtime during which it was laid out with long rows of tables and chairs.

It had a fully functioning stage at one end with steps going up to on it either side - and proper theatre curtains and back stage area - and lights and all that jazz, and this was used for regular stage performances of school dramatic productions and other events.

As far as I can remember, I performed on the stage twice during my time at the school – both around Christmas time.

In my first year I played the Owl in a lavish production of Alice In Wonderland. You remember the Owl, surely – a major role for an 11 year old...!

Me and John Giddings and a few other minor child actors who I don't remember played a group of woodland animals who had to dance a habanera (like they do...).

Unfortunately for us, the music teacher who played the piano for the music on the night of the first performance played completely different music to what we had been using in the drama studio to practice the dance routine with so that completely threw us.

If I recall correctly, we had three performances of the play in all and I don't think we ever got the dancing right in any of them.

The other time that I performed on the stage was for a big carol concert when we were in the sixth form – probably December 1984. Somebody had come up with the idea of putting together a singing group made up of sixth formers and teachers to perform some songs in harmonies.

A couple of my friends were involved – David Gilding and John Ludman – so, not wishing to miss out on any excitement, I went and joined in as well.

We practised for several weeks beforehand in the music room after school under the watchful eye of the then music teacher Mrs Whittingham. She was great fun, by the way, and also taught some of us sixth formers how to play basic guitar chords during what we used to call "frees" and what the teaching staff annoyingly insisted on referring to as "private study periods".

While I enjoyed the singing immensely, I was severely disadvantaged by the fact that the harmonies that we were required to sing didn't always follow the main tune - and I couldn't read music!

Luckily, I have a good ear and good memory for trivia and mimicry so, by sitting next to Mr Gilding who was singing the same parts as me, I eventually managed to learn my bits by copying what he sang.

The carol concert was a really big event, played in front of a huge audience in the main hall and accompanied by the school orchestra.

The majority of it was general carols that everybody in the audience could sing along to and there were also instrumental pieces and our bits.

We'd learnt several songs that I had never heard of before and got the harmonies off quite well.

These included "Adam Lay Y Bounden", "This Is The Truth Sent From Above", and "Personent Hodie" (sung in Latin) and we did a few lighter numbers as well such as "Penny Lane" and "Here We Go A Wassailing".

We also had a general school carol concert held at St John's Church in Stanground that year – where all the kids had to traipse down one afternoon. David Gilding's dad was the Vicar there – he was also great fun by the way – and I'm fairly sure that he made a recording of us singing our harmonised songs in the church that day – but I never got to hear how it came out.

The school had very good rapport with the church at that time and I recall that on the last day of term several of us heftier lads were required to help take down the huge ceiling height Christmas tree that had stood next to the stage in the corner of the main hall in the run up to the festive season, carry it outside and attach it to the roof of the Rev Gilding's estate car. It was then taken to the church and reused there for the Christmas period itself, which seemed a very good use of resources.

We also used the Main Hall when we had large numbers of pupils sitting exams – O Levels for example - and it was laid out with individual tables and chairs for this purpose.

But the principal use of the Main Hall and what we were in there most of all for was morning assemblies. These were different to what we'd had at primary school where we used to say prayers and sing hymns. We never once said a prayer or sang a hymn at a morning assembly in my time at Comprehensive school.

There were some 1200 or 1300 pupils at the school and by the time all of them were crammed into the hall along with all the staff members and 6th formers, it was quite a feat. The teachers sat on chairs along the sides and the 6th formers sat on chairs at the back but everybody else had to sit on the floor in carefully marshalled rows.

42

As such, we normally only ever had a full assembly with everybody attending once at the end of each term.

The rest of the time, we had different smaller assemblies on different days. I am sure there must have been some overall timetable to govern what took place when but we as children were never informed of this and just did what we were told on any given day.

In order to minimise the amount of chaos involved in bringing everybody in, the assemblies were held in particular groups and the information given out tailored to whoever it was who was there.

One day it was "lower school" – which was 1st, 2nd and 3rd years, another day it was upper school – which was 4th and 5th years and 6th form. We also had separate assemblies for "all girls" on some occasions and "all boys" on others, although none of these seemed to happen on a specific day of the week and it wasn't a regular weekly occurrence.

We also occasionally had "House Assembly" where all the people from one house met at the same time irrespective of year or gender and this was always held in the Small Hall.

These were held fairly infrequently – quite possibly once month – and I imagine were quite difficult to schedule because we had six houses in all (to find out more about the school houses, see Volume 3: Cricket & Baseball) and they had to be fitted round so as not to clash with the other assemblies in the main hall.

The Small Hall was also used for exams - either as an overspill or when there were a smaller number of people sitting a particular subject. I am fairly sure that I sat my English Literature O level exams in there. Everybody did English Language O Level but only the top class (ahem...,) did Literature, so that would make sense.

I also remember being in there when taking part in the inter-house speech competition and debating competitions - and it was also the venue for the after school judo club, and had all the mats stacked up in one corner when they weren't being used.

So – now you know what I mean by the Small Hall – and that is where we had our French Breakfast.

It turned out that Marks & Spencer's in town had started to stock French Croissants at the time. Not the scrumptious freshly baked ones that you can get now – just the stodgy ones in packets – but, even so, this was the first time that anybody could buy croissants in Peterborough anywhere so it was quite an exciting development around the languages department.

As we had been learning in our classes that French people had croissants for breakfast, and that they drunk their morning coffee out of bowls instead of cups - and that they wiped out the bowl with the croissant, it was decided that we should all be able to have an opportunity to sample this experience culinaire.

We were also told that they put chocolate spread on their bread, which I thought sounded absolutely revolting at the time but have since come to appreciate that Nutella can actually be quite pleasant on a piece of warm buttered toast...

Everybody who wanted to sample the French Breakfast had to bring in 25p the week before to cover the cost of the supplies and, on the day itself, we assembled in the Small Hall during morning break time.

This caused a bit of a fuss because normally everybody HAD to go outside during break times and lunch times - but some of the older kids who were stewarding the corridors (this was done by different houses on different days) hadn't been informed that we little ones had an important function in the Small Hall.

There were tables laid out and each one had a small plate with half a croissant on it and we were then served hot coffee out of jugs, poured into what were probably dessert bowls.

Needless to say, I really enjoyed this sophisticated continental experience and was very keen to discover more.

Which brings us seamlessly back to Quiberville-Sur Mer...

The Colonie de Vacances had a large indoor hall that we used on our last night for a disco but luckily the weather was nice for practically the whole time that we were there and we were able to spend most of the time outdoors.

There was a large closed yard round the back where we could play football but the downside to this was that there was an open gateway along the side. This led to a side road which had a very long steep incline and, if the ball went out there, you had to run like mad to try and retrieve it.

Once we had settled in at the Colonie, we were given some of our pocket money. This had been paid over by our parents before the trip and was being looked after by the teachers who had, presumably at some point beforehand, exchanged it for French Francs.

I seem to think that everybody had the same amount – so as to avoid arguments or showing off – and it was dished out a bit at a time over the course of the trip.

So, armed with our very exotic looking Francs, Gids and I decided to go off on our own and find "the shops".

We were walking around the quiet streets of Quiberville wondering where there might be some retail outlets when we came across two foreign –looking lads of similar age to ourselves. In my very best first year French, I asked:

"Où sont les magasins?"

They obviously understood this because they started babbling in animated response but, unfortunately, the bizarre regional patois that they were using bore absolutely no resemblance to anything that we had learnt in Mme Mercy's classes at school.

So, being English, and much frustrated that very first French people we had ever come across couldn't even speak French properly, we tried again with a slightly more forceful:

"Où sont les magasins?"

This must have worked because not long afterwards, we found ourselves standing outside what appeared to be the only shop in Quiberville - certainly the only one that we ever found, anyway

It stood on its own in an otherwise residential street and looked like somebody's house. It had the quaint French shutters open at the windows and were it not for the legend "Epicerie" above the door, and a few odds and ends hanging in the doorway, one might have gone straight past it.

It was very gloomy inside but it had the most fascinating array of fruits and vegetables hanging up in bunches around the walls - and the whole place had what I now know to be an artisanal garlicky smell.

Luckily, it was not so out of the way and traditional to not have bottles of coca-cola and chocolate bars on sale so we were able to emerge successful with our first transaction with foreign currency.

From there we wandered down to the beach that was a bit further down the road.

Looking at Quiberville seafront now on the internet, it looks like quite a nice place – with a promenade and beach huts and lots of tourists – but I don't remember it being like that at all. Admittedly, it wasn't really beach weather when we were there - and it was during the week (possibly at siesta time...) but I don't remember seeing anything much on or around the beach at all.

It may very well be that we were not on the main touristy beach at all – but another bit somewhere further along the coast. Let's face it, I doubt they would have built a holiday home for steelworkers' kids slap bang in the middle of the swishy tourist area – so that would make sense.

What I do remember seeing on the beach were rather un-picturesque lumps of old concrete. It turns out that these would have been left over from the Atlantic Wall defences that had been built by the Germans to defend the coast after they had occupied France in the Second World War.

There was also a huge concrete outlet of some sort (sewage, probably) that spurted water out at regular intervals into the sea. Not very sanitary, obviously, but of huge interest to your average 12 year old boy on holiday!

Above left: A view of the Arc de Triomphe in Paris from the window of our coach. Richard Ellis can be seen. Above right: The Palais De Justice.

Paris / Rouen

The most exciting part of our trip to France – in my opinion, anyway, was a day out in Paris.

I am fairly sure that this took place on Thursday 24th May 1979 as that was Ascension Day, and we stopped off in Rouen - which was on the way – to look at the cathedral.

I remember that, before we got off the coach, Mr Davies (Head of Languages at the time) warned us that it was a special day in the church calendar so there would be more people than usual praying in the cathedral and that we should not disturb anybody while we looked around.

Rouen Cathedral was very big and ornate and impressive and, as Mr Davies had said, there were a lot of people sitting or kneeling praying quietly to themselves. Not being a huge authority on religious architecture as a 12 year old, I didn't really take too much in about the building as such but I am jolly pleased to at least be able to say that I have been there.

After spending a short time at the cathedral, we got back on the coaches and continued on to Paris. To be honest, I think I was so excited about being there that the day in Paris is now a bit of a blur to me and I can't really remember much about what we did.

I know that we drove around on the bus for a bit – and then walked around for a bit and that we ended up at the Eiffel Tower. But aside from that, I am open to any reminders...

Dieppe Shopping

On another day, just before we came home, we had a day shopping for souvenirs and gifts in a larger nearby town. My guess is that this would have been Dieppe as that is only 18Km along the coast and is the only big town in the area that fits the description.

As I recall, it was a bit overcast and gloomy that day and John and I went into a cafe to order two coca colas. We were rather unceremoniously thrown out by the owner for reasons that our limited French never discovered and had to content ourselves with going into a small supermarket instead and getting a bottle of Orangina and some biscottes (French toasts).

Feeling really French after this, we went into one of the many souvenir shops and decided that we would buy breakfast bowls for all of our family members to take home. I can safely say that the bowls that I bought have truly survived the test of time as they have remained safe in the crockery cupboard at my mum's and she currently uses them for her breakfast cereal in the mornings!

We also looked in a record shop while dodging a shower and I bought a 7" single of Something Else by the Sex Pistols – just to be a bit rebellious.

We didn't actually call them 7" singles back then, by the way. It may well have been a record industry term but I don't remember hearing it until a few years later, once 12" singles became popular with the record buying public. And 45s - or singles – then became more widely described as 7" singles so as to differentiate between the two versions.

When I was little, a 7" inch single was usually referred to as a "45" – referring to its playing speed of 45 rpm, as these had replaced the old 78 rpm discs as the format for a record with a single song on each side.

You could also get "Long Playing" records which were 12" inches in diameter, played at 33 rpm and had about 20 minutes playing time on each side. These normally had 6 or 7 songs on each side and became known as albums.

So you had singles and albums but, as a hard up 11 / 12 year old, you only usually had enough money to buy a single very occasionally (albums came as Christmas or birthday presents) so when you said you were "going to buy a record", that is what you tended to mean...

It is worth pointing here that the record sleeve for Something Else features a cartoon drawing of Sid Vicious wearing a red t-shirt with a swastika on the front. As the swastika is a banned image in France, the cover of my record has him wearing a plain red t-shirt and no swastika, which makes it quite unusual.

And that's about all that I can remember about my first ever trip abroad. I seem to think that we travelled back on a day crossing on the ferry on the MV Leopard - which was more fun as we were able to stay out on deck most of the time and enjoy the trip more.

Record Sizes

12"

10"

7"

- Usually plays at 33 rpm.
- Plays at 45 rpm if an E.P.
- Holds around 22min of music per side.

- Usually plays at 78 rpm.
- Used to hold around 3min of music per side.

- Usually plays at 45 rpm.
- Holds around 5min of music per side.

(Explanation courtesy of www.vinylrecordlife.com)

The original sleeve design for Something Else – and my French sleeve with the swastika removed (all rights reserved ...). My record also had the centre missing - as was the case with many "foreign" sourced records at the time - and had to have an adaptor fitted so as to be able to play it on a domestic record player.

1982: Barneville – Carteret

I went on a school trip to Barneville-Carteret in Normandy on the north coast of France in the late spring of 1982.

I was originally going to go the year before but my dad had an accident at work and was off for a long time and there were concerns about money so it didn't seem the right time to be planning a foreign trip. Luckily they ran the same trip the following year so, in May 1982, off we all went.

In fact, on this occasion I can narrow down exactly the date that we went because the Scotland v England home international football match was on the television the afternoon before we had to meet up at the school – and that was played on 29th May 1982. England won 0-1 with a Paul Mariner goal, in case you are interested...

It was a nice sunny day as we set off and we must have been taking a night crossing to have left at that time. We sailed, I think, from Portsmouth to Cherbourg and the main thing that I remember is standing on deck and the sea was so calm, it was like the proverbial mill pond.

I wasn't usually a very good sailor and felt sick very easily but this crossing was by far the best I ever encountered. There was a big bright moon in the sky which reflected on the water. It was the most beautiful sight you could possibly imagine – just like something out of a film.

My friends and I were the oldest students on this trip – being in the 4th year (aged 15) by that time. The 5th years couldn't go as it was encroaching on O level exam time so we had extra kudos for being the oldest and most mature (supposedly) and, as such, we were given a bit more freedom and leeway to do what we wanted.

We stayed in a residential centre of some sort - but I don't remember what it was called, I'm afraid .... There are a couple of Centres De Jeunes listed on the internet, but at this distance in time, I can't really make out if it was one of those or not.

When you are taken somewhere as a group of youngsters on a coach, you don't take as much notice of street signs and directions as you do when you are driving and navigating for yourself as an adult.

Anyway, the residential centre had small dormitories with 6 bunk beds in each and we were assigned to those in groups of 5 or 6. I don't fully remember who went on the trip now but I do recall that we older boys – me, Paul Winskill, Alan Platt, Tim Wade and Darren Jinks all went in one room – and we had Darren's younger brother Andrew in with us.

As an aside - and I don't mean anything negative here but, as far as I can remember, hardly any of the other members of the trip were particularly good at French, unlike me (ahem...).

It was my best subject at school whereas others excelled in other subjects – Darren Jinks was good at maths and sciences for example, Alan Platt did A level English and History and so on. In fact, I am fairly sure that I was the only person who went our 1982 trip – certainly that I knew of anyway - who actually went to do A level French in the 6th Form. But in the overall general scheme of things, that's all a bit by the by..

Some of the other younger boys kicked up at this as it meant that "Pangie" - as Jinks minor was called for some odd historical reason that I was never party to – was allowed to hang around with us and have a later curfew time, even though he was the same age as them...!

This led to another minor bone of contention that we thought was quite amusing – but the little ones didn't!

There was a bar/cafe a little way up the road from where we were staying – probably about 10 minutes walk away.

I imagine that, as it is actually a popular tourist resort, there was a lot more in the main towns of Barneville and Carteret that we never got to see, but we were perfectly happy as we were.

Anyway, the first full evening that we were there, we all got dressed up – polished our shoes and everything – for an evening on the town. Well, an hour in the cafe up the road before bed time, anyway...

And because we were the oldest, we were allowed to go unaccompanied – and as Pange was with us, he could come as well, which annoyed the oiks even more!

So we walked up to this bar feeling all grown up and sophisticated. It was pretty quiet when we went in with just a couple of elderly locals sitting at the bar drinking little glasses of red wine.

They looked a bit like old fishermen out of Enid Blyton stories, which may well have been the case as the area had a thriving local fishing industry at that time.

The serving staff must have been used to bizarre groups of foreign students turning up as they were very welcoming and we sat around one of the tables and all ordered beers.

There was a group of local youngsters who we met up with a few times. They came and played football with us on the field at the back of the Centre (that's when we learnt the varied uses of the term "merde!") and they also tagged along when we went for a few after-tea walks in the surrounding country side.

The most memorable thing about this trip – and I might sound a bit laddish here, but this is how I remember it – was that there was a group of girls who were a year or so younger than us – and we all got on really well.

Although we all went to the same senior school, they were in different years to us and unless you happened to be in the same tutorial group with somebody, people from diverse years didn't tend to mix.

I don't know if it is the same now as it was when I was younger but it was generally accepted that most girls used to mature more quickly than boys and, therefore, found boys of the same age to be annoying. I can safely say that despite having fancied lots of girls from a distance during my school years, none of them ever gave the impression of fancying me back. So for anybody that did - and was maybe too shy to make an approach – I truly apologise....!

In the main, girls my age were usually attracted to boys a year or two older than themselves and most boyfriend / girlfriend couples tended to be like that. I, for my part, never fancied any 12 years olds when I was 14 so that was that really...

So suddenly we found ourselves as the oldest boys on the trip – going off to an exciting exotic location, in the company of a load of girls who we weren't hampered by having known since we were about 4 years old. Now I can tell you about this because nothing untoward ever went on - it was only harmless fun, nobody snook off anywhere – and sex hadn't been invented when I was 14, anyway...

So as it was all innocent hanging around together in a big group under the reassuring constant watchful eye of the teachers - and no snogging or anything like that, I feel quite happy in naming names.

The ringleader of this group of Pink Ladies was a girl called Helen Harrison. She was the one that first started talking to us when we were on the coach heading off on a day excursion somewhere. On the initial journey out to France we had just stuck in our own little groups of friends and didn't really mix very much.

At the Centre we all ate our meals around one big square of tables so the opportunities for getting to know the others were much greater.

When we got to wherever it was we were going on this jolly jaunt, we were introduced to the rest of the Pink Ladies and these were: Melanie Heugh, Clare Millen, Julie Blades, Alison Pavey and Lisa Zirpolo. So after that, basically what happened was that whenever we went anywhere, we'd all go around as a big group.

I don't think any of them actually fancied any of us but it was just a lot of fun.

Oh – and they weren't actually called the "Pink Ladies" either. That name comes from the film Grease and I just added it here for effect...

I saw Melanie quite a lot afterwards, in fact, in a purely platonic way - as she started going ice skating on Saturday nights. Another extended "member" of the Pink Ladies was Janet Crowson who didn't go on the French trip but did go ice skating so I got on vaguely friendly (platonic) terms with her for a while as well.

It's all a bit of a haze now with the passage of time - but over the course of the trip (I think we went for a week and two weekends so as to have the Whitsun half term away and not miss any school ...) but I certainly recall having the following trips out:

We went to Mont St Michel for the day. It was a really warm sunny day and there were a lot of visitors there. We parked down on a big car park and walked up the slope to the citadel.

The normandie–tourisme.fr website describes Mont St Michel as:

"a magical island topped by a gravity-defying abbey, the Mont-Saint-Michel and its Bay count among France's most stunning sights. For centuries one of Europe's major pilgrimage destinations, this holy island is now a UNESCO World Heritage Site, as is its breathtaking bay". And they are bang on the money there.

Having said that, Mont St Michel was featured in a French crime drama a couple of years ago called Temoins that was shown on Channel 4. It was set out of season and the place was all gloomy and miserable and practically empty. It was almost impossible to believe it was the same place that we had visited, although I imagine that's the same for a lot of touristy places in the winter.

My main recollection from being at Mont St Michel is sitting under a big table umbrella in a group at a cafe with outside tables looking out across a decorative court yard and marvelling at the wonderful medieval architecture of the place.

I was drinking a beer. I love French beer, as long as it's cold – although not so much the cheap Kanterbrau bottles you get in Hypermarkets - and the drinking age limit in France was 16 at the time and, with us being 15 or so, we were able to get away with ordering it.

Most of the girls were drinking coca cola or "diable menthe" which is lemonade mixed with peppermint cordial – a bit oversweet for my taste, possibly nicer with soda water - and you could also do the same with grenadine syrup (from pomegranates).

Our coach driver Keith was sitting with us and he introduced us to a citron pressé – which is lemon juice in hot water, explaining that it is much more refreshing than tea or coffee and, therefore, better for you in hot weather. I have that every morning now when I wake up.

Top Photo: (l to r) Paul Winskill, Julie Blades, Helen Harrison, Clare Millen & Melanie Heugh at Mont St Michel, May 1982

Left Middle: Alan Platt next to an American tank on the beach at Arromanches.

Left Bottom: Alan Platt, Paul Winskill, Andrew Jinks and Darren Jinks sitting on an abandoned landing craft at the D-Day landing beach at Arromanches in May 1982.

Another day we went to visit the D-Day landing beaches at Arromanches on the other side of the peninsula. This had been the site for the Gold landing beach that was used for the British forces troops on 6th June 1944 and subsequently served as the location for a Mulberry artificial harbour that was installed to disembark equipment and more troops in the aftermath.

It's quite a trek from Barneville-Carteret to Arromanches – 110km or so, according to Wiki Maps - but the journey was quite interesting through the pretty French countryside and the weather was nice.

We went past – but, unfortunately, did not stop at – Bayeux, home of the famous tapestry and also drove through Sainte Mere Eglise.

If you know your military history, you will know that this was a key route of defence for the Germans leading up to the American Omaha landing beach between at Sainte-Honorine-des-Pertes and Vierville-sur-Mer and, as such, needed to be secured so that the US troops could link up with the British troop arriving at Gold beach just along the coast.

Ste Mère Eglise was, in fact, the first French town to be liberated in the Normandy landings after 30 US paratroops were dropped there overnight on 5th/6th June before the main beach disembarkations began. The town is prominently featured in the film The Longest Day and is best remembered for the scene where the paratrooper gets snagged up on the church roof.

I don't know what is there now, but when we went to the beach at Arromanches, there were loads of bits of concrete and steel littered around the overlooking cliffs which will have been a part of the German coastal defences. There were also a number of discarded military vehicles and landing craft which had obviously been left there at the end of the war and were by then in a rusty and highly decayed state.

Despite the likely danger to human health, you could clamber all over these artefacts –which was great fun for your average 14 year old English visitor!

There's a great museum to the D Day landings at Arromanches – it's called "La Musée Du Debarquement" and it was opened in 1954 as the first permanent display dedicated the operation.

It is built on the site of Mulberry harbour that was installed there and you can apparently still see bits of it a few hundred yards out on the beach – although we didn't know that at the time of our visit.

The museum was really good to look round when we went in 1982 and, I dare say, with all the modern visitor features that are now available, it'll be even better today!

There were quite a few interesting things going on in the media when we were in France in May / June 1982. The Falklands war was in full swing and I regularly bought the French language newspapers to keep up to date with what was going on.

It was also the lead up period to the football World Cup in Spain, which England and France had both qualified for so there was a lot of coverage about that as well.

Music-wise, young German singer Nicole had won the Eurovision Song Contest a few weeks beforehand with the charming ballad "A Little Peace" so that was a big hit right across Europe at the time – and we were also being deluged with upbeat hit medleys like "Stars on 45".

I also seem to think that the video game Donkey Kong was the big thing in the arcades that summer. Not that I was ever a big games arcade sort of person but they certainly had it on the ferry when we sailed over and also in one of the cafes that we frequented while we were there.

So there you go – a few reminiscences of our 1982 trip to Barneville – Carteret in Normandy!

PB on the beach near Montpellier in May 1984 with (left to right) Fabienne, Odile, Isabelle, Cecile, Trang & Alice.

1983/84/85: French Exchange To Montpellier

Note: I went on the A Level French exchange to Montpellier in the south of France two years running - in 1984 and 1985. For the most part, the same people were involved on both occasions, so certain events may, over time, have got muddled up in my memory as to what happened when.

I shall, however, try and keep this account as chronologically correct as I can manage - and will attempt to explain any discrepancies as they crop up.

I am going to cover the French Exchange years all in one go here as it makes more sense. I do actually have another trip to France to mention that came up in August 1984 but will do that separately as it was a different sort of thing all together.

A rather poorly framed photo showing me, my brother Gary and French penfriend Nicolas at Ferry Meadows near Peterborough in June 1983

Summer 1983.

In the summer of 1983, I took part in the A Level France exchange at Stanground School. I knew I was going to do A Level French in the Sixth Form the following year but I ended up being out of step with the rest of the exchange people as I had my French student visitor a year early.

What would normally happen was that I would go and stay with my French penfriend in Montpellier at the end of May 1984 and the French students would come over and stay with us for 2 weeks later in the summer. Then we'd do the same thing again the following year – keeping the same host families – so that our French would be really good ready for our final A level exams in summer 1985.

However, in the run up to summer 1983, I was asked by the French teacher Mrs Roberts if I'd mind being teamed up with a French lad who wanted to come that year.

As far as I could work out, his year mates were a year above the kids who my group would be stopping with the following year – and the people they were coming to see were two years ahead of me just sitting their final A levels and I, consequently, didn't know any of them.

I don't really know how they came to ask me, particularly. I always liked to think it was because I was the best French speaker in my year group but, in reality, I think I was probably the best male French speaker in my year group who was going to stay on in the 6th Form and do A Level French, thus being there for the return leg of the exchange.

As far as I can remember, there was only me and Steven Garratt doing A Level French who fitted into that category. So it was possibly just a 50/50 choice and I don't actually know whether he was asked or not…

Anyway, I agreed to go along with it. So I went along to the railway station and congregated with the other host families who were waiting for the train coming up from London with the French students. There was another host family – a girl who lived just up the road from us. I knew who she was but had never spoken to her but I can only assume that my penfriend didn't know her girl visitor either as they never seemed in the least bit interested in meeting up while they were here.

So we had this French lad called Nicolas who came to stay with us for two weeks. His dad was some big noise in the local French sports / education facilities in Montpellier so had presumably pulled strings for Nicolas to come and visit out of step with everybody else.

The first thing that I have to say is that I don't know why Nicolas wanted to do the exchange and come to visit England. He didn't seem interested in doing anything and he never wanted to go anywhere.

I know for a fact from the experience that I had in the two following years of exchanges that the kids regularly met up together, had little parties at their host family's houses or went out on trips and visits together.

But for the whole time Nicolas stayed with us, he never once asked to meet up with his classmates or to go on any of the activities which I assume must have been arranged.

One evening, we were going to visit my grand-parents in Ramsey and I told him that it was in another town a short way away in the countryside – and the grumpy sod didn't want to go. So he stayed at our house on his own and watched telly while we went...

I know we went up to the school and played tennis on the school tennis courts a few times. We went to the cinema once to see the Monty Python film "The Meaning Of Life" but apart from that, despite my excellent memory for details and all kinds of trivia, I can't for the life of me remember what else we did for the two weeks that he was here.

There is a photo of us together taken at Ferry Meadows so we must have gone there a couple of times. Oh, and his English was really crap as well....

This first visit for the French students gave me the opportunity to meet Mme Garcia before the rest of my year group. She was the overseas students' English teacher and her English was very good, compared to most French people's...

She was quite old – late 50s properly – (although most adults seem "old" when you are 16...) and very smart and refined. She was going to stay with Mrs Roberts – that's our French French teacher and Mrs R told us that she had been well prepared and sent over a huge chest of medicine for all eventualities.

May 1984: Montpellier

So, fast forward to late Spring 1984 and we sixth formers were all ready to head off to Montpellier for two weeks. All the others had been allocated a pen pal and they had been writing to them to build up a good relationship before we arrived.

I had exchanged a few letters with Nicolas in the intervening period. In one he said that during the period when we were due to visit, he would be preparing for his exams and he "wouldn't have time to busy himself" with me so it might be better if I didn't go.

I thought "sod that pour un jeu de soldats…". Having gone out of my way to accommodate him the previous year and put up with him being a moody git and not wanting to go anywhere or do anything much, I was NOT going to let him mess up my exchange trip, which was very important for my A levels. So I told him I was going anyway.

As we were all going somewhere that we hadn't been before, the journey down was really exciting.

We got the train from Peterborough down to London, the underground to Victoria Station and then the boat train down to Dover. Mrs Roberts came with us. Her parents lived fairly near to where we were going to – Arles or Nimes or somewhere like that - and she and her husband were doing up a barn to use as a holiday home.

She was going to travel down with us on the train to make sure we got there ok and was then going to stay at her parents, with her husband joining her later.

The ferry crossing to Calais was uneventful and we then got the train to Paris which took about 3 hours. Once we got to Paris, we took the Metro from the Gare du Nord to the Gare de Lyon, which is where the overnight train to Montpellier would be leaving from. Because Mrs Roberts knew her way round, she suggested that we put our luggage in the lockers at the station and go out for a bit as we had a couple of hours before the train was due to leave.

We went to the Centre Pompidou and had a look around the square outside and then went and had a drink in a café.

Now, because of this, I can tell you the exact day that we travelled out there. It was 19th May 1984. And how do I know that? Well, it was the day of the FA Cup final and, by the time we had got to Paris in the evening, I hadn't heard what the result was.

In the bar where we went for a drink with Mrs Roberts while waiting for the night train, they had the French radio news on in the background and they were talking about St Etienne being relegated for the first time ever after losing the relegation play off to Racing Club de Paris.

So I very bravely went over and asked the barman in my not very good French if they had mentioned who had won "La Coupe Anglaise?"

Now – you know when you watch the FA Cup final on the television and they tell you that it is being watched live in 100s of countries around the world...? Well, I can tell you that France wasn't one of them. At least it wasn't in 1984 because nobody who I asked in that packed bar knew who had won the English FA Cup that afternoon!

I later discovered that Everton beat Watford 2-0, by the way... but, it does, at least, give me a clear marker to be able to identify the dates of the trip.

Then we went back to the Gare de Lyon, retrieved our luggage and prepared to board the train.

On this trip there were

PB – (penfriends: Nicolas Becourt 1984 / Guillaume Baille 1985)
Steven Garratt (Serge Aubague)
Joanne Harrison (Isabelle Dejoux)
Annette Piccaver (Capucine Olry)
Karen Goodacre (Fabienne Dance)
Diana Pacocha (Muriel Cazalis)
Karen Robinett (Alice Hennequin)
Julia Skelton (Cecile Gachet)
Jane Kon (Odile Merit)

To make up the numbers, there were also 2 girls from Arthur Mellows Village College – which was a school in Sawtry a little way down the A1 from Peterborough.

Julie / Sarah Carroll (penfriend unknown)

Mara Radjenovic (Trang - Vietmanese...?)

Those of us who had been to Southfields Junior School already knew Julie Carroll (she calls herself Sarah now but I have never been able to get used to that...) because she used to live in Stanground and went to school with us until age 11.

Her mother re-married somebody called Darke and they went to live in Stilton so Julie went to a different secondary school when we started in September 1978.

Interestingly enough, Mrs Darke – who knew me, as I had been to their house a few times when we were little – was the Office Practice teacher at our school and she was also the tutorial (registration) teacher in the room next to the one I went to so I saw her quite often.

But it was still a bit of a shock to suddenly see Julie / Sarah again, having not seen her for 6 years or so.

Anyway, we all had couchettes booked for the overnight journey to the South of France. These were set up in the compartments that were used for normal seating during the day and, unlike Poirot's luxurious sleeper berth on the Orient Express, these were six to a cabin and it was rather basic.

You had a pillow of sorts and a sheet / blanket and you slept in your clothes - but it was certainly more comfortable than sitting up all night – or those reclining chairs that they have on ferries.

Considering the strange surroundings, I actually did manage to get a bit of sleep on the overnight journey. However, the train shuddered and jolted every time that it stopped and there was a bit of shunting and uncoupling at certain stops as well.

Every time I woke up I looked out to see where we had stopped and it really was a fascinating journey.

These days they have a direct fast TGV route from Paris to Montpellier that takes about 4 hours but they didn't have that back when we went.

They still have an overnight Inter City service even now, though –
leaving Paris at 22.20 and arriving in Montpellier at 9.30am – a
journey of 11 hours or so.

Once we got past Lyon, it started to get really interesting and the
stops sounded more and more exotic: Vienne, Montelimar, Orange,
Avignon, Nimes and, once it got light, the architecture was so much
different to what we had been used to in the north of France.

The houses were all painted white. They had heavy shutters over the
windows and many had flat rooves and terraces. The fields were arid
and the local agriculture was completely different and when we got
off the train at Montpellier, despite it being quite early in the morning
and mizzling, the weather was noticeably warmer.

*****

Several of the host families from our group lived in a village called St
Gely du Fesc which is to the north of Montpellier and a few others
lived in Castelnau le Lez – on the east of the city. Le Lez in the river,
by the way, that runs through Montpellier into the Mediterranean at
Palavas les Flots. It is pronounced "Les" and not "Lay" as one might
expect from normal French pronunciation.

My host family – the Bécourts lived in a village called Pérols which is
to the south of Montpellier on the way to the beaches.

His mother was the bursar or some sort of pastoral manager or
nurse or something at the College de Pérols, which was the
equivalent of a junior school and, because of this, the family lived in
a flat at the entrance to the school grounds. They were on the
ground floor and I think the caretaker was on the upper floor.

They were actually building their own house down in the village and
Nicolas's dad Jacques took me to have a look at it a few times over
the course of my visit.

Anyway, it turned out that my arrival had caused an unexpected
amount of upheaval in the Bécourt household as Nicolas's little
brother Alexandre – about 7 or 8 at a guess, that annoying age
where they whine a lot – had to share with Nicolas so that I could
sleep in his room.

Nicolas – as I already knew – was working hard preparing for his exams and wouldn't have time to "busy himself" with me and he certainly wouldn't have wanted to hang around with the rest of my group who were younger than him – and that suited me just fine. I didn't have to go with him to school and I was basically able to pick and choose what I wanted to do.

I did have to meet up with him for lunch on the first day at school – Lycée Joffre in Montpellier – and I was actually supposed to lunch with him every day so that, I suppose, his dad could pay the bill.

I met him outside the réfectoire and he had two friends with him. He very cursorily introduced me as his "corres" (that's short for correspondent , ie French for penpal – they abbreviate things a lot in French...) and then I had to rush to keep up with them as they navigated their way around the food counters.

Now, I don't really know what else was on offer as I didn't get a proper opportunity to check out the day's menu or look round the full selection of serving counters but I ended up with a plateful – or rather not full at all – of the most awful watery undercooked steak that I have ever seen (I didn't dare to ask what it supposed to be a steak of…) and some lentils and not much else.

After this very disappointing experience of French cuisine, I went into the town centre and found to my relief that there was a McDonalds – so I filled up on cheeseburgers. They actually call a cheeseburger "un cheeseburger" in McDonalds in France - but they give it a heavy French pronunciation, ie "shaysboorgair". Plus they also served beer!

The next day, I skipped the "starters" at the Lycée réfectoire all together and went straight to the McDonalds in Montpellier centre.

One good thing that did come out of being Nicolas's correspondent and him living in Pérols was that I was located much closer to the coast / sea than the other penpals were.

So as not to leave me too cut off from everybody else, it was agreed that I could borrow his bike and go for long bike rides along the coast on my own while the others were all attending lessons at the Lycee with their own penfriends.

As well as the busy main road along the coast, there were also little roads that went along the coast connecting the beaches – signposted "Carnon par les Plages" and "Palavas par les Plages" and so on - and this is the route that I took on my explorations.

The montepllier-france.com tourist office website describes Pérols as:

8 kms south of Montpellier, a stone's throw from the Mediterranean sea, Pérols spreads along two salt water lakes: the étang de l'Or to the East and the Mejean to the West. An unusual location which forges the history of this village and gives exceptional panoramas.

And I can assure you from personal experience that this is the case. It is the most beautiful place you can possibly imagine. I expect that it will have seen a lot more development since I was there but the views across the water and along the wetlands are absolutely stunning.

As it happened, there was a huge Carrefour Hypermarket on the main road through Pérols so, once I had Nicolas's bike, I was able to pop in there when I felt like it – to get drink or a crafty snack and, later on to buy French records that I had heard and taken a liking to and other things as souvenirs and presents to take home.

For the first of my biking expeditions, I cycled eastwards along the coast to La Grande Motte which is a modern tourist resort built in the 1960s and 70s with very avant garde architecture. According to Wiki Maps, it is 14 km to La Grande Motte so, taking that both ways, it was quite a trek.

Another day, I went in the other direction and headed for Palavas Les Flots, which was not so far – just 7 Km in each direction. That was a completely different experience as the place was really quaint, old fashioned looking and rustic.

There was a very pleasant bar / restaurant along the coast road that I stopped at whenever I went past - to have a little mid excursion refreshment.

It was actually in the middle of nowhere and there was nothing else around it. Whenever I went in there was never anybody else there – I imagine it got busier in the evenings – and the lady behind the bar seemed quite amused by this bizarre English bloke who came out cycling in the in mid-day heat.

I seem to think that it was called Le Mas du Petit Près – "mas" being a traditional Provence word for a farmhouse – but haven't been able to find mention of it anywhere on the internet. There is an area of beach along there called Petit Travers, so it might have been called that and I have just remembered it wrongly.

Anyway, surrounded by the sand dunes and with sand being blown across the road surface by the famous Mistral wind, the place looked like a scene out of the High Chaparral!

PB with Nicolas's bike – at the Lycée Joffre in 1984

Recent photo of the Domaine de Pailletrice winery at Pérols, taken from their Facebook page. (Photo by Jé Denice)

French Wine

On the 21st May 1984 (I know this date for a fact as I still have the document that I am going to tell you about), I went out with Jacques to buy some wine.

This wasn't just a bottle of wine from the Hypermarket down the road, this was locally produced artisanal stuff and he went to buy it straight from the farmer /viticultor who produced it.

It was a local vineyard on the edge of Pérols, less than a mile from where I was staying, and the guy had the wine stored in some sort of big underground vat. You couldn't see the wine or the vat, there was just a large hump in the ground with a tap sticking out from it - like a water stand pipe on its own in the middle of a yard.

And from this tap, he filled large containers with whatever quantity of wine the customer wanted to buy.

Now, "Frenchman Buys Wine From Wine Producer" shock! I know what you're thinking – this isn't anything unusual in itself. But by being party to this little escapade, I did learn something quite unusual.

In order to go and buy a quantity of wine of 3 litres or more, you had to have to have a special licence to transport it home!

So I have kept this special document safe in my possession for 37 years – just so that I can now tell you about it. I didn't know if it is still like this now but they were, apparently, very strict about this at the time.

This restricted licence allows the holder to transport the alcoholic drink listed from the address of the supplier to their own home and nowhere else.

You couldn't just pick the wine up and then go swanning off for the day doing other things – there is actually a time limit marked in on the document showing how long it is valid for on the day of issue.

In this case, the licence was issued at 6.45pm and was valid for 1 hour.

It even goes so far as to specify the number plate of the vehicle that the purchaser is using to transport the booze!

The wine producer here is called Carrière and they are still going today. The vineyard – called the Domaine de Pailletrice – has been in the same family since 1954, before which it had been a private estate and a chapel before that.

According to their website, the Pailletrice has an area of 50 hectares and grows a variety of different vines - Carignan, Alicante, Sauvignon, Merlot, Syrah, Chardonnay and Grenache. The best crops are kept cut short to improve the quality of the wine and are aged in oak vats.

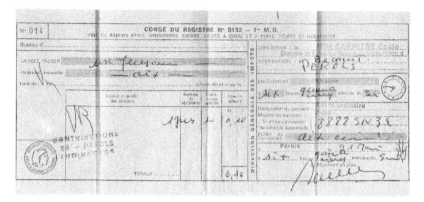

Licence allowing the transportation of 0.10 HL of wine (ie 10 litres) on 21st May 1984.

Aside from the bulk quantities that you take away in containers, they also have their own range of bottled wines, have a showroom, run tasting sessions and have won lots of prizes over recent years.

French Family Sunday

When I first started visiting France, nothing much happened on a Sunday. The shops weren't open and most people spent time with their families. As such, I was able to experience a typical French Sunday at home with my host family.

We had a big family meal at lunchtime but, before that, we had an aperatif. A popular drink in the Bécourt household was Pineau de Charentes which according to its Wikipedia description is "a fortified wine (mistelle or vin de liqueur), made from either fresh, unfermented grape juice or a blend of lightly fermented grape must, to which a Cognac eau-de-vie is added and then matured".

You can actually buy it now in England in all sorts of places like Sainsburys, Waitrose – even Lidl – but, back then, it wasn't something that I had ever come across.

There are, actually, different types of Pineau from different areas. This one wasn't from the Montpellier area at all but from Charentes – in the west of France towards La Rochelle.

I wasn't a big fan of wine or liqueurs at that time - I suppose it is a taste that you develop more as you get older. But I did like the French beer.

This Pineau, however, was rather pleasant. It was quite thick and sweet – like a clear version of port or sherry – and was a very nice start to a meal on a warm sunny day.

The meal itself was great. The mother (whose name I have forgotten - I'm really sorry, Mme Bécourt...) brought out a huge dish of mixed salad with a wonderful dressing, boiled eggs and fresh baguettes and I thought to myself "what a good idea for an easy meal on a warm day...!"

So I had a goodly supply of that and really enjoyed it. I was ready for dessert. But she took that away and brought another huge dish – this time full of meat - with vegetables to go with it.

I'm afraid I don't know now what the meat dish was, although I am sure it was very nice. I was in a bit of a shock as I was already full on the salad and this had taken me somewhat by surprise. It's my own fault, I know, for not having paid more attention.

Now, the "modern-day me" would have been all over the kitchen, getting in the way, "helping" with the preparation of the meal:

"Ooh, Madame – what is that? How do you do that? What do you call this?" etc

but back then I was a typical 17 year old English male, very shy, and rather insecure in my temporary surroundings - so I didn't.

So I have no memory now of what it was or what else we had. I know that it was all very nice - and very copious, especially for me as I hadn't paced myself properly.

We had freshly ground French coffee afterwards, which was also a new experience for me. I always had "Twinings English Breakfast" tea in the mornings, which they had found in the Hypermarket for me – and the coffee helped to counteract the effect of the Pineau and the wines that accompanied the meal.

I bought a packet of the Carte Noire coffee to take back to England with me but, as we didn't have a coffee making jug or a percolator at home at that time, it never got used.

I don't know whether they had it on every week or not but on Sunday afternoons when they showed live coverage of the Formula 1 Grand Prix, they used to have a programme on French TV called "Champions" and it went on for much of the afternoon.

It wasn't a purely "sports" programme as such as they also had guest interviews with non sports people and they also had singers on the show. One particular afternoon I remember they had Plastic Bertrand singing the French version of Peter Schilling's European-wide 1983 hit Major Tom.

I have always found Formula 1 racing to be a good way of breaking down barriers with other nationalities due to the many different drivers and teams who take part.

In the 1990s, for example, I enjoyed a fierce rivalry with my German girlfriend's Schumacher supporting family while I was cheering on Damon Hill. And back in the 1980s we had Nigel Mansell while the French had Alain Prost – who finished second in the 1984 world series despite having won more individual races than eventual champion Niki Lauda of Austria.

Also on Sunday, they had Starsky & Hutch on French television, which pleased me greatly as it was something that I already knew and having seen all the episodes in English, I had no trouble following the French language dialogue.

This was the first time that I had ever seen an English language programme dubbed into a foreign language and I found the voices really annoying as they tended to sound completely different to their English equivalents.

I have to say that I am a bit of a purist where telly is concerned - and even more so with Starsky & Hutch. For example, I much prefer the original theme tune they had for the first series – the menacing gloomy one - rather than the silly bouncy one that they used for the later series.

With the French version, it is even worse as they have a theme song. Yes they do! It starts off "Starsky et Hutch! Des nouveaux chavaliers au grand coeur" and so on. You can actually see it nowadays on YouTube by searching for "Starsky et Hutch générique".

Talking of génériques Françaises, there is one TV theme from that period that I did enjoy and that was Albator 84 – a kiddies' cartoon about some sort of space pirate. There again you can find it on YouTube. I couldn't say much about the episodes but I do like the title song.

They used to show quite a few English language programmes dubbed into French when I visited France in the 1980s and it was a good way of getting used to hearing French without over taxing myself with trying to understand a difficult story line.

They used to have The Persuaders ("Amicalement Votre" en Français), Miami Vice (Deux Flics a Miami), Hunter ("Reek 'unterre") and things like that – and, for odd some reason, the French used to be really mad over Benny Hill!

I have lost count of the number of times when, upon hearing that I was English, some zany French person has replied saying "Ah – Eeeengleesh! You like Beneee- ill....?"

Our other French teacher at A Level – Mrs Thompson – who once, albeit unwittingly, encouraged us to go and watch an incredibly smutty French film at the Peterborough Library Film Society – used to tell us that French people would always ask "Why did you burn Joan of Arc?", to which the clever reply was supposed to be "Because we were cold" (Parce-que nous avons eu froid...).

Unfortunately, to my ongoing disappointment, nobody in my whole life has ever asked me this question so I have never been able to try out that response.

Another TV show that they had on and which I could readily appreciate was La Chasse Aux Tresors - the original French programme upon which Channel 4's Treasure Hunt was based.

The English version – if you've never seen it - had the decorative Anneka Rice in various brightly coloured jumpsuits flying around interesting locations in a helicopter against the clock trying to find clues to some hidden treasure.

The French version when I saw it had a similarly decorative male as the "skyrunner" as they used to call the role. He was apparently an adventurous journalist called Philippe de Dieuleveult and he disappeared mysteriously while on some assignment in Zaire in 1985.

I have since watched an awful lot of television in France - and in Germany - and now that my language skills are much improved, I never watch any dubbed English programmes any more as I find the voices so very annoying.

Luckily I am now able to follow quite easily the majority of French, German or Italian domestic programmes – apart from the occasional slang term – and the modern wonders of Satellite TV, YouTube, livestreams and DVDs mean there is no shortage of material to watch.

*****

For the uninitiated, a French Lycée is a High School. The traditional French lycée covers the last three years of secondary education.

There are two main types of lycée - the lycée général (or lycée classique) and the lycée technique.

The Lycée that we exhcged with in Montpellier was named in honour of General Joseph Jacques Césaire Joffre (1852 – 1931), a French army officer who was Commander-in-Chief of French forces on the Western Front from the start of The First World War until the end of 1916.

He is best known for regrouping the retreating allied armies to defeat the Germans at the strategically decisive First Battle of the Marne in September 1914.

Here's a nice photo taken by Steven Garratt of most of the exchange group from Montpellier in 1984. I wasn't here for this occasion but it is nice to see the rest of them. Back row left to right: Serge Aubague, Alice Hennequin, Karen Robinett, Mara Radjenovic & Diana Pacocha. Next Row forward (5 girls together, from middle going right): Fabienne Dance, Isabelle Dejoux, Trang, unknown, Sarah Carroll. Front row (on steps): Annette Piccaver, Odile Merit, Cecile Gachet, Karen Goodacre, Jane Kon. Front (seated on floor): Julia Skelton, Joanne Harrison, Capucine Olry.

I think this photo was taken at the Lycée Joffre (school) which was where all the French students attended. Our group went to a few lessons with them to get the true French scholastic experience but I was at a disadvantage here because my French penpal was in a different year in a different part of the Lycée and didn't want me hanging around with him.

While that suited me as I was able to go off and do what I wanted, it also meant that I did miss out on the activities that the rest of the group did when they were together at the Lycée – or at least arranged while they were together.

Place de la Comédie, Montpellier, with the Fountain of The Three Graces, May 1984. (Photo by Steven Garratt)

The focal point of our socialising during the daytime (we didn't go "out" in the evenings – it's not something that young French teenagers used to do, apparently ...) was the Place de la Comedie in the centre of Montpellier.

All the local people called it the Place De L'Oeuf as that was what it used to be called and it was, apparently, shaped like an egg.

La Place De L'Oeuf is one of the largest pedestrianised areas in Europe and, from photos on the Montpellier – France.com official tourist office website, it still looks very similar to how it was when we were there.

It was easy to get to and there were lots of cafes where we could sit outside and enjoy the warm May weather and meet up with the others.

On one corner was the Gaumont Cinema that we went to on several occasions and across from that was a Quick (French chain) hamburger restaurant, which I also remember trying.

Also in the Place De L'Oeuf is the McDonalds where I ended up on numerous occasions.

While we were in Montpellier, we went to the cinema as a group several times. It wasn't an organised trip as such but a number of us decided to meet up and go together.

The first film that we saw was "Un Dimanche A La Campagne" which had recently won an award at the Cannes Film Festival and elsewhere and was highly regarded. And it was the most boring thing I have ever seen in all my life. Nothing happened in it as far as I can remember.

I do appreciate that it was supposed to be a film about a day in the country - and the dialogue was all in proper French without subtitles, which most of us would not have been used to listening to - but very little happened in this film.

I'd probably enjoy it if I watched it now but, at the time, most of we English students were happy when it was over.

Another film that we saw was "Notre Histoire" and that was much more entertaining. It was a romantic drama starring Alain Delon and Nathalie Baye - and then there was another one about some crooks who were planning an audacious robbery of a casino in Monte Carlo.

That was called "Les Specialistes" and I'm sure that we saw it in 1984, but, according to IMDB, it wasn't released in France until March 1985 so maybe I am wrong on that.

One afternoon we had a group meet-up on the beach (at Carnon, I think it was...) and we all took food and had a picnic.

One really interesting trip that we all took as a group was to the source of the world famous Perrier water and its bottling plant at Vergèze –which is about 40km away from Montpellier in the direction of Nimes.

On the way on the motorway, we were fascinated to see the sea turned red around the historic town of Aigues Mortes where there are unusual salt deposits that colour the water.

The name actually means "dead algae" and the Salins du Midi salt company that refines the salt now has a visitor centre and plant tours where people can go and find out all about it. I doubt it was like that when we went otherwise we might have visited there as well.

Anyway, it was fascinating to visit the home of Perrier mineral water and we had a guided tour around the factory. They also produce Orangina and a few other brands and we were able to see the process right through seeing the finished bottles being packed for dispatch.

Odile Merit adorning a statue of François Gigot de la Peyronie (1678-1747) - who was a famous pioneering surgeon born in Montpellier – at the old Faculté de Médecine. (Photo by Steven Garratt)

A recent photo of the bullfighting at Pérols. This photo is taken from the montpellier-france.com tourist office website. I did take some photos when I was there but they didn't come out very well. This shot gives a much better idea of how the event looks.

Ascension Day

Joanne Harrison has kindly reminded me that the majority of the group went on a hike up Pic St Loup on Ascension Day – which was Thursday 31st May 1984.

Pic St Loup is a mountain to the north of Montpellier and, according to Wikipedia, it is 2159 feet above sea level (658m) and has a hermitage, old chapel, cross & watchtower.

From the photos that I have seen, it must have a really impressive view of the surrounding countryside and other nearby mountains.

I didn't actually go on this excursion – partly because I didn't know about it and also because it turned out that my host family wanted to take me out themselves.

Looking back, I seem to remember that it was very hot and sunny that day, so an energetic yomp up a mountain with very little shade would probably not have been the best thing to do!

So, instead of having an afternoon of stunning views and mountain air I went to see an afternoon of.... BULLFIGHTING!

Yes – it's true. Bull fighting used to be very popular in the South of France – like it was in Spain - and they still have big arenas all over the place. Even the tiny village of Pérols had its own venue – Les Arènes De Pérols.

I had been assured that they didn't actually kill the bulls anymore and that it was just a bit of light entertainment – known as Bloodless Bull Fighting. So, not wishing to miss out on a southern French cultural experience, I agreed to go along and see what it was all about.

It turned out that they didn't have matadors with capes and swords, luckily, and the event was populated by young local lads. What they did was tie a bunch of ribbons (called a "raset") across the horns of the bull and these lads had to try and grab the ribbon off the bull without getting knocked over and trampled.

After a while, the bull got fed up with people rushing round it and the crowd cheering and it decided that it'd had enough and tried to get back out through the gate it had come in by.

The crowd thought this was hilarious for some reason and cheered all the more as the bull became more and more distressed. In the end I was secretly hoping that a few of the lads in the arena would get lightly mauled, just to even the score up a bit...

I don't know how long this went on for – how many rounds there were with how many bulls – and I don't remember if anybody managed to secure the prize off the bulls' horns, and I don't really care to be honest.

It was the most disturbing, distasteful thing I have ever seen and I couldn't for the life of me understand what everybody else could see to enjoy in it.

What surprises me even more is that they still do the bullfighting at Pérols and elsewhere across the South of France to this day – over 35 years later!

A travel website called The Culture Trip .com published an interesting article on this topic in May 2017 called An Introduction To The Bullfighting Season In Provence and I have reproduced a few extracts from it here as they help to put this phenomenon into perspective.

They are actually talking about events staged at Arles in a bigger arena than the one I visited - but the principle is very much the same.

"The Course Camarguaise does not end with the death of the bull. This type of bullfighting is from the Camargue region of France (southwest of Provence) and involves men, called raseteurs, trying to pull ribbons off the bull's horns. Unlike Spanish bullfights, the men are rarely injured and the bull is never killed.

Six bulls are normally used in each show, with the most agile and prized bulls going last. The bull is tired out during lots of chases, where the raseteurs jump over barriers to escape the charging animal. At the end of each act, music from the opera Carmen is played.

Awards are given to the best bulls, raseteurs, and bull farms. The bulls are led in and out of the arena and the best raseteur is allowed a kiss from the girl who has been crowned Queen of Arles for the day."

"Bulls are used in most festivals in some way or other in the Camargue, and are very respected. In Spanish bullfights, the matador is king and is always the star of the show. In the Camargue it is the other way around, and the bull is the most respected star. Training to become a raseteur starts in the early teens and is a prestigious job in small towns.

The French government has tried to ban bullfighting in the past, but faced so much local opposition in the south of the country that it backed down.

"Bullfighting is taken seriously and both kinds have special protection. In some places, cows are used instead of bulls.

The bulls used in the Course Camarguaise are bred especially for the purpose and kept in herds. Each fight lasts an average of 15 minutes, and then the bull returns to his herd, and might not be used again for a few weeks.

The 'star' bulls might fight about half a dozen times each year. They usually retire at age 14 or 15, when they are left out to pasture until they die. They are buried upright with their head facing the sea.

Travelling Home

The trip home at the weekend was rather fairly uneventful – in so much as an exciting rail journey across the whole of the length of France could ever be uneventful – just ask Agatha Christie!

We got the late night train from Montpellier and did the journey in reverse order, arriving at the Gare de Lyon in Paris early to mid morning. From there, we got the metro round to the Gare Du Nord – and probably had a spot of "petit dejeuner à la gare" at some stage before boarding the train to Calais.

As I recall there weren't enough free seats available on this service so we ended up all sitting in a baggage car part of the way but the number of passengers thinned out as we headed further away from Paris and we eventually all managed to sit together in proper seats later on in the journey.

Having said that it was uneventful, I seem to think there was a delay in boarding the ferry at Calais when we got there. This meant that loads of people all got squashed up in the departure hall and, being in big group, we erected a sort of corral with our luggage and sit in the middle of it having a picnic.

So, anyway, the REST of the journey – ferry to Dover, train to London, Underground to Kings Cross and train to Peterborough - WAS uneventful and I can't really remember anything particular about it.

And that was the end of the first leg of the 1984 French Exchange to Montpellier.

Photos on next page:
Top: Mara Radjenovic on the night train to Montpellier (Julie Carroll in the background) and Cecile Gachet at the social evening in the Stanground 6th Form block.
Middle: Isabelle Dejoux and Fabienne Dance in Montpellier
Bottom: Alice Hennequin and Capucine Olry at Karen Robinett's house

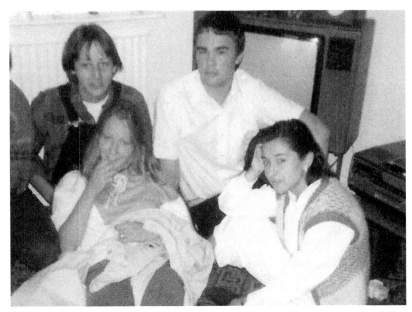

Watching France win the European Championship final on video at our house. Odile, PB, Capucine and Isabelle. Serge's arm is also in shot.

1984: Peterborough

When the French students came over for the second leg of the Exchange in June / July 1984, I was at a bit of a disadvantage as I didn't have anybody coming to stop with me. But this did, at least, mean that I could dip in and out of the activities - and that suited me quite well.

From what I remember, there was a lot of hanging about in Queensgate and going around town during the daytime.... and there was a day trip to Norwich on the train that we all went on – where I remember looking around the Cathedral.

There was a social evening in our Sixth Form block at school where we had a few bottles of wine and music to dance to on the record player – and some of the English host families also hosted social evenings at their houses as well.

I remember going to Annette Piccaver's house in Farcet one evening where we all had a nice evening in their large garden. We also had a evening at Karen Robinett's in Oakdale, and then on a really warm summery Friday evening, we had a barbecue outside at Joanne Harrison's – who lived a bit further up Coneygree Road from where I did.

However, despite not having anyone to look after this time, I still pulled my weight in the entertaining stakes.

While they were over here, the UEFA European Championships were being held in France and, not surprisingly, the host nation reached the final. This was played on 27th June 1984 and they beat Spain 2-0 to win the trophy.

As we had recently acquired a video recorder by that stage (VCRs were still not standard household accessories in the early 1980s...), I recorded the match in full and the next morning a few of them came round to watch it.

Also, Steven Garratt had a university admissions interview at Selwyn College in Cambridge one afternoon and I went with him on the bus and looked after Serge while he was ensconced.

I even got myself up early on the Sunday morning to go and see them all off at the railway station when they were about to go home. Both Mrs Roberts and Mme Garcia commended me for my dedication as they hadn't expected me to go.

There were 3 of us who did A Level Italian – and here are the other two thirds of the class: Karen Robinett and Diana Pacocha.

But I'm like that...

April / May 1985: Montpellier

The second year we went to Montpellier was a bit different as not all of the same people went.

Several of the girls from the previous year didn't go and we had some lower 6th French students come with us – David White, Rachel Manley and John Baker are the ones I particularly remember – but there may have been some others as well.

We also had three new girls from (I presume...) Arthur Mellows Village College who were friends of Julie/Sarah Carroll. These were Corinna Solomon, Michelle Henderson and Cathy Whiting so there was a whole new batch of penfriends to get to know and this was a bit awkward as the new ones were all a year younger than the original ones.

Following on from the previous year's debacle, I had a new penpal – Guillaume Baillé who was the same age as the younger ones. He was best friends with Pascal Dalmesso who was David White's penpal so at least it meant that we would be able to mix with the others on a more of a joined up basis than the previous year.

Now, date-wise, I can't quite work out when it was that we went over there. I thought it was the end of May like the previous year but looking at my writing on the back of some of my photos, I have written "April 1985" so it must have been earlier than I thought.

The journey down was very memorable - but for all the wrong reasons. Mrs Roberts didn't travel down with us this time – and I was put in charge of the group rail ticket.

Something happened when we were on the ferry crossing and our ferry was very late in docking at Calais. Apparently there had been some sort of collision earlier in the day and it had put one of their berths out of action and everything else was backed up as a result.

This meant that we ended up getting a later train from Calais to Paris than we were scheduled to get, that we arrived later at the Gare du Nord and by the time we had rushed across Paris in taxis to get to the Gare de Lyon, our overnight train to Montpellier had already left.

We asked a station employee what we could do and he told us that there wasn't another one until the next morning. I found a payphone and rang Mme Garcia, as I had been given her home phone number for such eventualities, and told her that we had missed the train and would not be arriving in Montpellier early the next day as expected.

She said that she would pass the message round to all the host families and wait to hear what we got fixed up with in the morning.

Now, I would probably have handled it completely differently if a similar situation arose today but, back in 1985, there were no mobile phones, no internet, no 24 hour amenities and nobody to ask.

There wasn't anywhere still open on the station concourse where we could go and sit or have a hot drink or anything and, not really knowing our way round and not wanting a load of young people to be traipsing aimlessly around Paris in the dark with a load of luggage, we decided to camp down in a corner of the station, slightly out of sight of the main thoroughfares - and away from any draughts, and wait for the first train next morning.

We were somewhat reassured as two policemen came along with a police dog to find out what we were doing. Steve and I explained to them what had happened and why we were stopping in the station - and they said that was OK as they would be patrolling round but that we had better not venture out into the streets on our own, just in case.

By the time we had got back from talking to the policemen, Diana and Julie had gone off on their own to find a late night bar to sit in – so our numbers were reduced and I now had them to worry about as well.

Luckily, they came back after an hour or so and we all sat on the hard floor of the station talking and dozing. The weather was pleasant so it wasn't overly cold but, needless to say, I hardly slept a wink and felt absolutely dreadful the next morning.

At first light, (sunrise is something like 5.30 am in Paris at the end of April...) we gathered our things together and went back onto the main platform area where we bagged a couple of the benches so that we could sit normally again and wait to see what train we could catch.

Although I felt awful and had hardly slept, seeing the station gradually open up first thing in the morning was quite an experience.

Just as it was getting light, the early morning employees started arriving, then the cafés and stalls began opening up and there was the smell of fresh coffee, warm croissants and Gauloise cigarettes in the air.

The first commuters started to arrive and the first trains moved off for the day.

Once the station toilet facilities had opened up – manned by the obligatory grumpy old woman demanding 50 centimes entry fee - we took it in turns to go and ablute and then go off and grab some breakfast while the others looked after the luggage.

The first train of the day that was heading in the direction that we wanted to go was the TGV express service to Lyon.

There is now a direct TGV service all the way to Montpellier but there wasn't back then and it only went as far as Lyon. But we would have more choice of getting local connections to our final destination from there, so it was worth a try.

I asked the chief conductor for the train if we could use our ticket on it (knowing full well that we probably couldn't as there were big signs up everywhere saying things like "TGV - Tarif Exceptionel" and "Reservation Obligatoire") and I explained our predicament.

He was very sympathetic to our plight and said that, while it wasn't exactly legal, he would let us come on the train – but that all the seats were reserved and we would have to stand in the door ways.

If it had been just me on my own - without a load of luggage - without 10 or 15 other people to worry about - and not having just had the worst night's sleep of my life.... I might have jumped at the idea but common sense prevailed and I figured it would be better for us to wait for the first regular train of the day that we would all be able to sit down on and catch up on some shut-eye on the 6 or 7 hour trip down to Montpellier.

Luckily, the trains actually started their journey at the Gare De Lyon so they were already standing there waiting for quite a while before they were due to leave.

This meant we had the advantage of being there before the rest of the travellers and were able to get on early and suss out which seats didn't have reservation tickets so that we could all sit more or less together.

I don't remember what time our train left now – it's all a bit of a cloudy haze. It was probably about 8am in the morning but, when you have been up all night and sitting around waiting since the crack of dawn, it already felt like the middle of the afternoon...

Anyway, we found out what time we were due to arrive in Montpellier – and that WAS going to be sometime late afternoon – rang Mme Garcia to let her know and then we were finally able to take our seats on the train.

I can't tell you much about the journey down through France as I was dozing on and off for much of the time. That was a shame as I would really have loved to have been able to see the different towns and cities that we went through in daylight for a change - and to watch the gradual transformation of the agriculture and the architecture the further south we travelled.

Anyway, by the time we reached Avignon – an hour or so out from Montpellier – I had perked up a bit and started making the obligatory jokes about "dancing on the bridge". That's a reference to a traditional French song "Sur Le Pont D'Avignon", by the way...

So it must have been mid to late afternoon when we arrived at Montpellier station and Mme Garcia and all the host families were there to meet us. So far as I remember, we went to Guillaume's and had something to eat and a restful evening.

He lived alone with his dad, Jean. I seem to think that the parents were divorced and I never heard anything about the mother...

They lived in a very nice flat in a district on the north of Montpellier called Le Plan des 4 Seigneurs - which is an unusual name that makes it very easy to remember, even after all this time.

This was close to the campuses of the various universities in Montpellier, which made sense as Guillaume's dad was a University lecturer – although I don't remember what in (certainly not English...!).

It was at the end of a bus route which made it handy for us to get into town to meet the others and it was easier to identify which bus to get back home again afterwards.

We hung around at the Lycée quite a lot and played a bit of tennis invariably losing quite heavily, and met the others in town from time to time but I certainly don't remember ever going to any lessons – so the French education system remains a mystery to me to this day....

As I mentioned previously, French kids didn't seem to go out very much in the evenings so, while we went out and did things during the day with our penfriends and in groups, the evenings tended to be very much stay at home affairs.

In the Baillé household, Jean did the cooking when he got back from work at the University – plain single dad stuff mainly nothing overly gourmet chef but, obviously in France, even "plain single dad stuff" was rather nice!

After the meal we all tended to watch television and there were a couple of programmes that they liked to watch, both comedies.

"La Bébête Show" was a French political satirical show - a sort of mix between the Muppet Show and Spitting Image - and there was also a programme called "La Famille Bargeot" (bargeot or bajot is a French slang term for "crazy").

This wasn't very popular on French television, apparently, and it only ran from March to June 1985. They were short 13 minute episodes and it was on TF1 everyday from Monday to Friday at 7.40pm before the main 8pm news.

The Baillé household – me included – watched it every evening and I quite enjoyed it – but there you go...

After the news, there was always a film on one of the channels, so we often watched those until bed time.

When I was there at that time, the main channels were TF1, Antenne 2 and FR3, which had regional variations and they also had Canal+ which showed some programmes unscrambled but you had to subscribe to watch films etc. Other channels like TV5 and M6 came along a few years later

PB at Foix in the Pyrennees, April 1985. This photo looks a lot clearer in reality than it has reproduced here, but at least you get the idea! (Photo by Guillaume Baille)

Visit To The Pyrenees

For the middle weekend of my 1985 in Montpellier, we went to Foix in the Pyrenees mountains to visit Guillaume's grandparents for a few days. That was quite a journey as it represented a drive of around 250 Km which would normally take 3 to 4 hours depending on the roads and the traffic - but for us it took considerably longer because Jean's car broke down half way there.

We had to get towed off the motorway and ended up in some tiny little village that had a car garage and not much else.

The mechanic couldn't say how long it would take to get the car fixed, as he would probably need to get some parts delivered, so it was agreed that we would hire the brand new Citroen BX estate that they - rather fortuitously – had parked outside.

This was really swish – with loads of room inside, electric windows, cassette player and all sorts of things that hadn't been present in Jean's old Renault - so it was quite a treat to make the rest of the journey in it.

The journey itself took us past / through some really interesting places. We went past Sête, Cap D'Agde, Béziers, Narbonne and also the fascinating medieval citadel of Carcassonne.

Foix is in the capital of the Ariège department in the Occitaine Region and was a very pretty place. Ratter quiet and out of the way - but certainly nice for a visit.

Guillaume's' grandparents had a large old fashioned house and were very welcoming.

His grandfather had, apparently, been in the resistance during the war and, while I am sure that is true, I'd imagine that EVERYBODY would say that their relatives had been in the resistance during the war – as going around saying that you were descended from a collaborator would NOT make you very popular...

He was a bit deaf and didn't speak very clearly so I had trouble communicating with him but I chatted quite a lot to his grandmother – who was a wonderful cook by the way.

When his grandmother spoke, I was able to detect what I came to realise was a southern French accent. It was quite subtle but would come out in certain words - like when she asked whether I had flown to Montpellier and I said we had taken the overnight train, she referred to it as "le trenn" rather than le "trang", which is the normal metropolitan French pronunciation.

French Rugby

While we were in Foix, we went to watch a rugby match – which was probably a Saturday afternoon.

In France they call what we call Rugby Union "le Rugby" and Rugby League "le Jeu de Treize", to avoid any confusion, and this was a Rugby Union game that we went to see. I don't remember who Foix were playing but it was a cup game and they won – and it meant that they would play Orange in the next round.

It was a lovely warm sunny afternoon, and with me being used to English weather, I think I was just wearing a t-shirt and probably had a light jacket with me in case of draughts.

We met up with Guillaume's grandfather on the way out of the rugby ground and I gathered that, as an old doyen of the town, he had been watching the match from some VIP enclosure somewhere.

But the thing that surprised me the most was that, while I was already wilting in the Pyrennean spring heat, he was wearing a jacket, cardigan, tie, overcoat and hat – more clothes than I probably wore at home in the middle of winter at that time! That was a great illustration to me of the huge difference in climate.

Now, the Baille family was very much a rugby family. In fact, every family member that I met – grandmother, uncles, whoever - upon hearing that I was English, said that they had "been to England once" – and that was to see a rugby match. Whether they all went at the same time or went to different matches separately I never found out.

Guillaume's dad (I think he was called Jean... but can't quite remember...) was a keen rugby player in his youth and round the family home in Foix there were numerous black and white team photos with him in them.

Of course, the modern day sports writer version of me would have made more of an attempt to enquire about these ie which team - what year - what competitions - what trophies etc ... but I was very quiet and shy back in those days.

Interestingly enough, while we were staying in Foix, they had a rugby related film on TV on the Sunday afternoon. It was a French black and white comedy – at least, I think it was black and white, but a lot of people still had b/w televisions in France in those days – and, despite clearly being a French film, it featured Diana Dors, Bernard Cribbins and Arthur Mullard.

It's about a Frenchman who travels to London to watch a rugby match (England v France) and, due to a comic set of circumstances, he gets into all sorts of mischief.

We all sat and watched the film together, which was nice, and I pretty much understood it all as it was basically standard Ealing Studios humour, albeit in the French language.

I have never seen this film on English television nor does anybody else ever seem to have heard of it, making it a bit of an oddball. So I looked it up on the good old internet and apparently it is called "Allez France" in the French original.

It was released in 1964 and written and directed by Robert Dhery – who also played the bumbling lead character. According to the IMDB, there is also an English language version, called "The Counterfeit Constable" – which as I say, I have never come across. Diana Dors plays herself in the film – which probably won't have taxed her too much...

Château de Montségur

Another day while we were in Foix, Guillaume, Jean and I went to see the ruins of the chateau at Montségur, about 30km away out in the mountains.

This was originally the site of a razed stronghold of the Cathars (Catharism was a Christian religious movement that thrived in the south of what is today France in the 12th to the 14th centuries) although the present fortress was actually built in the 16th century.

The chateau is right on the top of the mountain at 1200m (3900ft) above sea level and it can only be accessed by a steep rocky path which leads 170m up from the car park.

We were actually very lucky on the day we went as it was a cloudy, overcast and not especially warm. There was a light mizzle in the air some of the time and that made it much more comfortable for the rather energetic ascent up the steep path. Had it been hot and sunny like the day we went to the rugby match, it would have been unbearable in the open on the side of the mountain.

While not overly busy as such, there were still quite a few other visitors around and, in places, you had to stand aside to let people pass on the path as it was so narrow.

Legend has it that Montésegur had been the resting place of the Holy Grail and that it was spirited away by 4 Cathar priests just days before the castle was overrun by forces loyal to the Pope in 1244.

It certainly was an interesting place to visit. The mountain air was so clean and fresh - and the views from the top of the surrounding area were absolutely stunning – even on a gloomy day.

Back In Montpellier

While we had been away in the Pyrenees, a bit of controversy had been stirred up in Montpellier as a fun fair had arrived in town and set up in one of the leafy squares.

The local council didn't want them there but seemed to be powerless to remove them, so, instead, they parked municipal vehicles all round the square – buses, dustbin lorries, cherry pickers, you name it – all squeezed very closely together to try and prevent people going in.

But I can tell you from personal experience that this tactic wasn't 100% successful. The slim-line 18 year old me was able to follow much of the rest of our group squeezing between the nose to tail council vehicles to go and joy all the fun of the rather empty fair!

*****

One evening when we were back in Montpellier, they arranged a social evening of some sort at a local youth club.

It was a pleasant enough event and nice for all the English and French to get together as a group in the evening for once. Cécile Gachet was also there – one of the French penpals from the previous year – and it was nice to have a chat and a dance with her.

101

But – there was pas d'alcool and the music was very "French orientated". By this, I don't mean it was all French pop songs – I would have preferred it if it was, to be honest - but it was all the music that the French kids were into – Bruce Springsteen's "Born in the USA", Joan Jett's "I Love Rock n Roll" etc - none of which was very good for dancing to.

I honestly got the impression that most French kids at that time wished they were American...

Now, as I mentioned before, the French kids didn't used to go out on their own in the evenings so they all thought this brilliant.

Whereas we Englanders were a bit more used to a less sheltered existence back in good ole' Peterborough. I know for a fact that several of our group used to go The Still at weekends (that was a long standing traditional real ale pub in the centre of Peterborough than attracted a rather trendy "Bohemian" clientele...) and we also regularly had pub lunches at the Whittle Way to celebrate people's 18th birthdays when we were in the 6th form. But they had laid it on for us – so what can you do...?

One interesting thing that came out of it was that we were all given a badge that said "Touche Pas A Mon Pote" which was the slogan of an anti-racism campaign that was very big in France in 1985.

From this, as well as finding out about the campaign, we also learnt that the word "pote" was a French slang word for "mate"!

Coming back to the rather odd musical tastes of the French, my wife Lucy – who has spent considerably more time in French speaking countries than I have – has this theory:

"It has to do with the shape of our jaw line, the muscles of which form due to our mother tongue - the language we learn from birth. Unless you speak more than one language before the age of 15, your jaw muscles become set and it therefore becomes very, very difficult to speak another language, however well you know it. These muscles also affect the ear canals and that, in turn, affects how you hear sounds."

This theory explains very clearly why French people – unless they were brought up bilingual from birth – always have a strong French accent when they speak English, however good their vocabulary and grammar may be.

I don't mean this in a nasty way at all, but I have never once come across a French person who spoke accent free English. You could always tell they were French as soon as they opened their mouths.

That's not to suggest that my French is perfect by any means. I have a certain level of fluency in the spoken language and a university degree but I daresay that a native speaker would easily detect my deficiencies from a mile away. In fact, I have it on good authority that most French people can pick out an English person just by looking at them.

You compare this with, say, Germans, or Dutch or Scandinavians who on the whole tend to speak better English - and often without an accent – or, at least, not an accent that you can necessarily identify as being from a particular place.

*****

"Beverley Hills Cop" starring Eddie Murphy was the big summer film hit in France in 1985 and we all went to watch "Le Flic de Beverley Hills" as a group at the cinema in the centre of town.

La Grotte De Clamouse - The White Corridor, the most magnificent part of the Cave, full of aragonite Crystals (Photo by Martin Souchay / Wikipedia)

La Grotte De Clamouse

One day we all had a trip to the Grotte de Clamouse – which is a stunning underground cave full of huge stalagmites and stalactites about 40 minutes drive north of Montpellier.

I seem to think that it rained all day long but, as the cave visit was mostly underground, it didn't really matter.

The Grotte is near to a village called St Guilhem le Desert - which I always thought was an incredibly odd name for a village – but it means it has stuck with me all these years.

Wikipedia describes the place as "essentially a medieval village located on the Chemin de St-Jacques (Way of St. James) pilgrim route to Santiago de Compostella.

In 804, the count of Toulouse and Duke of Aquitaine Guilhèm (Saint Guillaume) founded a monastery here at a time when the valley was virtually uninhabited, hence considered "desert".

The abbey was originally called The Abbey of Gellone, until after Guillaume died in 812 when it was named The Abbey of Guillaume, and then the Abbey of Saint-Guilhem after his canonization in 1066.

We were supposed to have gone and had a look around the abbey in the afternoon but the weather was so bad – torrential rain all day long - that it was decided not to bother attempting it.

Instead we spent all afternoon sitting in a cafe and had a very nice surprise when Mme Mercy – my first French teacher from Stanground popped up out of nowhere to join us!

I have to say that, with the awful weather keeping all the tourists away, and all the locals safely indoors, the village of St Guilhem really did live up to its name that day!

*****

So, all good things must come to an end and we had to head home after a fantastic two weeks spent in the south of France.

Would you believe that I don't remember a single thing about the journey home - apart from arriving back at Peterborough station in warm sunshine on a Sunday late afternoon.

Now, quite how anybody can manage to not remember a journey of some 830 miles, across the whole length of France from south to north, via two important world capitals with their relative underground railway networks, on four separate trains - and with a sea ferry crossing in between, I have no idea. But there you are...

So nothing awful can have happened, anyway...

Photo left: Visit To York – Guillaume, Fabienne, Sophie & Steve. Photo Right: Guillaume on a punt in Cambridge – both June 1985.

June 1985: Peterborough

So in June 1985, the final leg of what had begun for me two full years earlier in June 1983 kicked off and the French exchange students arrived on the train from Montpellier.

I am pleased to say that Guillaume fitted in a lot better than the previous one had done and we did lots of socialising with the other students - and also went out on several group trips.

We went to Cambridge for the day on the bus and I distinctly remember the normally cool, suave and unrufflable David White having a stand up row with the bus driver when we wanted to come home again as he had said that our ticket wasn't valid for his bus and we'd have take a later slower one.... It was a very hot day as I recall so tempers could easily be frayed...

The highlight for me of the trip to Cambridge was that we all went punting in the river and were able to take in the spectacular views of colleges.

We had lunch in a pub down by the river and saw the rowing crews swishing by in the water training.

I also have a few photos in my possession that were taken by Steven Garratt (he had a better camera than I did so his photos always came out better) of a trip to York and the Castle Museum.

Now, while I remember perfectly well going on a trip to York on the train with the school in the 2nd Year juniors – where we visited the Railway Museum, The Castle Museum and also walked around the historic city walls – I do not have the slightest memory of going to York with the French students.

As I do not have any photos of my own from this trip – and do not feature in any of Mr Garratt's either - I can only assume that I didn't go – which begs the question "why not"?

Guillaume went - so why didn't I?

And if I did, why can't I remember it?

Answers on a postcard, please...

*****

One of the weeks of the French Exchange visit, my old friend from school Mark Eastwood had time off work. He had started off in the Sixth Form with us (I can't remember what subjects he did) but then left to go and work for Barclays Bank.

I had passed my motorbike test earlier that year and was allowed to carry passengers and Mark also had a motorbike so we went out for several nice afternoon rides in the surrounding countryside, with me taking Guillaume as a pillion passenger.

One day we went to Ferry Meadows and played pitch and putt even though none of us was actually any good – but it was nice and sunny and an enjoyable way to spend the day.

At Mr Baldwin's Party, June 1985. Photo left: Kathy Whiting (left) and her French penpal Sophie. Photo right: Guillaume with Steven Garratt.

Mr Baldwin's Party

One event that I do remember very well was a social evening at Mr Baldwin's house.

Mr Baldwin was the head of English at our school and he, along with Mr Forster, taught our English Literature A Level classes - and he always took great delight in explaining all the bawdy bits in the Chaucer tales and Shakespeare plays that we were studying.

I don't actually know what this party was for. Back then - as I have mentioned previously, everything didn't get explained to you like it does now with the internet and Facebook and whatever. You were just told to be somewhere at a certain time and that was it. We were told "Party at Mr Baldwin's house – be there!".... so we were.

Now, don't get me wrong – we didn't go off hobnobbing with the teachers on a regular basis and certainly never went to their houses.

When I was at school, if you saw a teacher out in the street – or in a supermarket – or wearing jeans instead of a suit or jacket, maybe out with husband/wife and children, you'd tend to stare at them if they had just arrived from Mars.

Because you normally only ever saw the teachers within that closed environment at school, you never imagined them doing anything else.

Certainly not having fun - and it was quite difficult to imagine that they even had first names, as they always used to refer to each other as Mr and Mrs so and so in front of us.

So this was definitely a one–off, at least for us - even if it wasn't for the teachers.

In fact, it wasn't **technically** a one off as I remember, at the end of our final year in the Sixth Form – which this was – a few of us were also invited to Mr Hoyle's house out in a country village somewhere.

This was a drama related event and there was just 6 of us who had been involved in the drama productions who had been invited.

This is nothing whatsoever to do with the French exchange, by the way, so do bear with me...

It was a delightful dinner party with Mr Hoyle who was head of drama and his partner Sue Gaskin – who we knew already as she had been, and still was, a teacher at our old Southfields junior school.

There's a bit of a common thread here, I'm afraid, as I can't quite remember who else went. Unfortunately, everything that went on during spring and summer 1985 when I was supposed to have been concentrating on my A Levels has become merged together in a sort of Bacchanalian haze...

I know that I went - and I know that John Ludman went. I am fairly sure that Alan Platt went (as we were all the main male characters in the Romeo and Juliet play that we did during the year).

There were also 3 girls there to balance the numbers - Annette Piccaver, Julia Skelton and Joanne Harrison (recently confirmed to me) – to make it 6 guests and two hosts around the table.

It was a very nice meal that we had – I'm afraid I don't remember exactly what it was but Miss Gaskin (sorry – that sounds very Jane Austen, but that's what I am used to calling her. I couldn't possibly call her Sue – even though we were asked to...) was a very good cook and a wonderful hostess – and there were wonderful wines to accompany it all.

I specifically recall Miss Gaskin saying how much she preferred a dinner party where everybody could sit round and all talk together rather than a noisy party where little groups congregated in corners (she might not have said that last bit - but it is certainly the gist of what she meant...) - and I agreed totally, and still do.

Looking back, Joanne commented to me about the dinner party: *"Yes - it was very sophisticated. I think they were trying to teach us manners! It was a lovely evening."*

Indeed, that evening was the first time that I had been invited to something like that. We lads dressed up and wore jackets and ties - and it was a very special occasion, so much so that I still have fond memories of it some 36 years later!

Anyway – back to the party at Mr Baldwin's house. This definitely was the sort of party where people congregated in little groups around and about the place.

It was a lovely warm summer evening at the end of June and the front and back doors were open and people were wandering in and out (by that I mean party guests circulating and mixing, obviously, not gatecrashers and random passers-by like you might get nowadays...) plus it was in Stilton which is pretty rural – so it was a really relaxed atmosphere.

The caption on the back of one of my photos says 27th June 1985, which was a Saturday, but I thought this was a Thursday evening - so who knows...?

As I said earlier – I'm not exactly sure what the particular occasion was for this party.

There was a whole mix of different people there – we were there with the French students and a load of teachers had bagged the comfy chairs in the living room.

Mr Baldwin was there, obviously, and I think Mr Forster, Mr Jones (history teacher), Mr Barker (headmaster) and, with it being in Stilton, I would imagine Mrs Darke was there as well.

There may well have been other teachers there – and their spouses - but we youngsters, still feeling rather awkward about the teacher / student thing back then, mostly kept away from the living room and populated the rest of the ground floor.

Alan Platt was certainly there, so there must have been an English element to the guest-list as he didn't do the French exchange – and I remember him quite clearly having some convoluted and highly animated conversation with Kathy Whiting, who I don't think he had ever met before, on the stairs.

*****

There was also a party at Simon Barks' house. Now this was - I'm pretty sure - on a Saturday evening. He was a year older than me and lived a bit further up on Coneygree Road. I can't quite remember whether this was 1984 or 1985 – and Simon was not actually in the Sixth Form, so I am not really sure how this event came about or how I came to be at it.

I seem to think that he was probably studying at the Technical College as I recognised a few of the other guests from when I had been to student discos there. He may have been doing languages there as I seem to think his mother was of Italian origin.

I am not even sure if the rest of the exchange group were there or not. All very odd!

It was a warm summer evening and my only recollections are of

sitting in the back garden, rather bored, and noticing the slight difference in view of the neighbouring houses and adjoining gardens from what we normally saw from our own garden a few doors down.

I seem to think that I was babysitting Serge – for some reason – but he really didn't need any looking after. He was the centre of attention in the garden and was spouting forth about how wonderful the proposed "United States of Europe" was going to be as a strong political and economic entity...

Reggae Scarf & Tea Pot

Talking of babysitting Serge, I remember another occasion when I had to go into town with him as he wanted to do some shopping. Don't ask me what Steve was doing and why I had to go - but that's what happened. Here again, I am not exactly sure if this was 1984 or 1985 as I have no recollection of Guillaume being around at this point so it may well have been 1984.

Serge wanted to buy a reggae scarf – the colours of which are, apparently, based on the Ethiopian flag, with red representing the blood of martyrs, green the beauty of Africa, and gold the wealth of Africa.

While you can buy absolutely anything from anywhere in the world now via the internet, I didn't know of anywhere that you could buy a reggae scarf in Peterborough in 1984 /85. Certainly not in the middle of summer when it wasn't scarf weather... The market, maybe – but that was only open on certain days of the week.

In any event, they certainly didn't have any in Woolworths, which was where we ended up – as, indeed, most people did in those far off halcyon days – and where Serge came up with the brilliant idea of buying a tea pot as a present for his host family.

I was fairly sure that, being a typical English family, the Garratts probably already had a tea pot and I did try to dissuade him in this venture.

But I didn't have any special insider knowledge in this regard. For all I knew, they could have dropped their one and only tea pot that very morning and smashed it into a thousand pieces with me knowing nothing about it. So in the end I had to oversee a rather stubborn Serge purchasing a rather large and heavy tea pot to regale them.

Needless to say – already having cupboards full of all the necessary crockery for tea making, they were "overjoyed" at this unexpected gift of yet another tea pot – which didn't fit anywhere and didn't match anything - and I got a good ticking off out of earshot for "letting him" buy it...

And so ends my association with the wonderful city of Montpellier on the south coast of France.

I travelled through it once on the train in 1987 and every bone in my body ached to get off and spend some more time there.

But it was the middle of the night and I was in the middle of a long and convoluted journey. I was also in the wrong company and it all was all wrong all round and wouldn't have worked. So we just chugged on through.

I did actually have the chance – not once but twice - to go back to Montpellier in 1997 when I was studying degree level French at University in Preston.

We had to spend the 1997/98 academic year in a French speaking country as part of our course and I managed to secure a "stage" at the regional Midi Libre newspaper there. It actually turned out that the newspaper was on strike for all the time that I might have been there so I wouldn't have had to do anything and could have spent my time rediscovering the coast and the nearby resorts.

As well as that, our University had a formal exchange arrangement with the Université Paul Valéry in Montpellier so I could have gone along with the other students from my year and attended classes there.

Unfortunately, my girlfriend at the time was German and it turned out that she was about the only person from the whole of northern Europe who didn't want to go and spend a year in the South of France. So in deference to her, I arranged instead to work with a media company in the Grand Duchy of Luxembourg where they use both French and German languages – as well as Luxembourgish – and would you believe, she didn't even go there with me either...!

So, aside from that rushed train journey in 1987, I have never been back to the south coast of France since 1985 – I would probably find it too hot for me nowadays anyway – but at least I have some very pleasant memories!

1984: Port Grimaud

This is a little bit out of sequence but I thought it was better to keep all of the French Exchange material from 1983/4/5 together in one place. So, now we back-step a year to 1984 and hear about when I went to St Tropez!

You know how there is a famous saying when people refer to "Brighton" and then qualify it by adding, "well, Hove actually."…. Well, this a bit like that as the holiday I went on in 1984 was to St Tropez – well, Port Grimaud actually.

I can tell you the exact dates of the trip as well - 11th to 25th August 1984. That has stuck indelibly in my mind after all those years – far more so than for any of the other trips I have ever been on. I can only assume that it is because it was the first grown up holiday that I went on my own and that it was the first time that I had arranged it all myself.

When I say I went "on my own", I didn't actually go "on my own". I went with my friend from school John Giddings, who I had known since I was 11 and who I had also gone motorcycle camping with the year before. On my own in this context means that it wasn't an organised school trip or a holiday with other family members.

We had originally wanted to go motorcycle camping again – on bigger motorbikes - and tour around the north of France. But John's dad talked us around to the idea that it would be better – and quite possibly cheaper overall - to fly to the south of France, get a fixed campsite there and just go out on excursions when it suited us.

We ended up booking a package holiday via EuroCamp – or somebody like that - through the Lunn Poly travel agents in town which included return flights to Nice, transfers from the airport, 2 weeks self catering in a family sized tent, and we also paid extra to hire a "kitchen package" which included a small gas stove, cool box, crockery and pots and pans.

So, on the day in question – which we all now know was 11th August 1984 – we took the train down to London, got the Underground round to Victoria Station and then boarded the Gatwick Express.

This was the first time that I had ever been on a plane and I found the whole thing very exciting. We were booked to fly on Dan Air which, in my youthful ignorance, I imagined to be the National Carrier of Denmark, all nice and swish like British Airways - but with very blonde stewardesses.

It turned out that we were actually flying on Dan-Air instead of Danair and that hyphen makes quite a big difference. Dan-Air was a London based company which, at that time, flew lots of charter flights to touristy destinations - and our flight at midday on a Saturday was, obviously, full of tourists on various package holidays.

Not that any of that bothered me. It was my first time in a commercial airliner and my first time flying abroad anywhere and I enjoyed every single minute of it – apart, maybe from the bit when you initially leave the ground and everything goes a bit "whoosh"...

Nothing overly eventful happened on the flight over – apart from the odd glimpses of things down below – and us buying some duty free booze - and we eventually arrived at Nice Airport. These days Easy Jet fly from Gatwick to Nice and the flight takes almost exactly 2 hours, so I imagine it would have been similar back then.

If you haven't flown into Nice Airport – and let's face it, some people might not have... – you might be interested to know that it is built sticking out into the sea. As you come in on your final approach, it really looks until the very last minute as you are going to do a "splash down" in the water like the returning astronauts in the space exploration craft used to do before the Space Shuttle was invented.

Anyway, we landed on terra firma, retrieved our luggage and were guided aboard a very nice French tourist coach with tinted windows and air conditioning.

This was almost full by the time that we left the airport and it dropped little clusters of people off at different stops along the coast. Nice to Port Grimaud is about 100 Km by road, which takes an hour and a half with normal driving, so you can imagine how long it took with regular stops and people having to get their cases out of the boot etc.

But it was a really interesting journey in itself and we went through many of the famous resorts of the Côte D'Azur – Antibes, Cannes, Fréjus and St Raphäel.

Our campsite was on the edge of a small town called Port Grimaud. This was half way between St Maxime and St Tropez and faced onto what was known as St Tropez Bay. Although it LOOKED like a quaint old fashioned place, most if it had only been built in the 1960s to cash in on the Brigitte Bardot – style attraction of the region.

Looking on Google and Wiki Maps, although I had forgotten in the passage of time, I am fairly sure that we stayed on the campsite "Holiday Marina". The name is vaguely familiar and it looks to be in the right location on the map. Looking at the various websites and reviews, it still looks very similar to when we went.

We were welcomed onto the campsite by the English site rep Gary – who allocated our tents and showed us what was what.

It was quite a big camping site – with different areas for different groups. We were in an area with static family sized tents that were used by package holiday companies. There was an area with static mobile homes / chalets that was used by Club Cantabrica – and was a bit of a step up from what we had in terms of comfort - and then there was a space a bit further away for casual visitors to arrive and pitch their own caravans and tents.

The site had a grocery shop where you had to get to early to get fresh bread each day and a bar / function room called The Bullseye – which did, in fact, have dart boards inside.

There was an outdoor swimming pool – pleasant enough and a decent size but just an ordinary one, with deck chairs and sun loungers all round.

From the photos of the place, now they have improved the guest amenities no end – but people are more picky these days than they necessarily were in 1984...

Anyway, after we had settled in, all the new arrivals were invited to a group meeting where Gary told us about the various events that were available over the course of the week.   Some people were only stopping for a week so they repeated the same programme every 7 days so that nobody need miss out.

For the benefit of posterity – and so you get an idea of the sort of things that people in the 1980s liked to do on holiday, I will list the events that were available as best as I can remember them.

There was a day trip to Ventimiglia just over the border with Italy. Ventimiglia actually means twenty miles in Italian and it was so called as it used to be 20 miles from the French border. I went on to change trains there on my epic train voyage in 1987, but we will come to that later.

Apparently with it being a border town – back in the days when countries still had proper borders – there was a thriving market there where you could buy all sorts of things cheaply – leather goods, duty free and whatever...

Now, with 20M (let's call it that to save ink...) being a two hour coach drive from Port Grimaud – and two hours back, I really didn't fancy spending 4 hours on a coach to go and look at some cheap stuff that I probably wouldn't want that was miles away from where I had come to be on holiday at. Some people might like that sort of thing – and I might have considered it later in the year when it wasn't beach weather.

So we didn't book up to go on the day trip to 20M.

There was also an excursion called the Booze Cruise – which was probably as revolting as it sounds. Apparently you'd go off in a small group of 6 or 8 people out into St Tropez Bay on a boat and it would moor in a secluded cove somewhere away from the main drag and you could jump off and swim in the warm water, and snorkle and look at rocks and fish and stuff.

So far so good...

Oh - and there would be an unlimited amount of booze available. Oh dear.

So we didn't go on that either.

As I am not a very good sailor, nor was I a very experienced swimmer, the idea of being stuck on a boat with loads of boozy people for several hours didn't really appeal. Had it been one of those huge luxury yachts like arab princes have – where you could sun bathe on a nice sun deck – with a glass of champagne or a nice chilled rose – or some sophisticated cocktail, fair enough, but a few crates of beer on a little cabin cruiser? Nein danke.

We later heard from somebody who did go on this that it was a rather small boat and it rocked a lot as people jumped on and off - so I think we made the right decision.

Something in the back of my mind makes me think that this trip took place on a Thursday each week. And I think it was cancelled the second week we were there as that was the day of the big tropical thunderstorm – which we will come back to later.

A Typical Day

As I mentioned earlier, in order to get to the beach, you had to walk out along the main road towards Port Grimaud. This was pleasant and tree lined for the first hundred yards but then turned into a sticky dusty expanse of concrete and tarmac for the rest. According to various tourism websites, it's approx 1 km to get to the town - ie just over ½ mile - and I seem to think that the beach was a little beyond the town centre.

Anyway, it was a good 20 minutes / half an hour yomp to get to the beach so once you got there, you tended to stay for the day.

If you went in the other direction on the main road – towards St Tropez, there was a big Casino supermarket and I know that a lot of people from our site used to walk there to get provisions and large cases of beer.

Once we had found out where everything was, we fell into a standard routine for the daytimes, which was pretty much as follows:

Waking up and abluting before breakfast. The toilets/ washing facilities and shower area were a couple of 100 yards from where our tents were so you had to have a modicum of clothing about you to make that trek – even though it was warm and sunny early in the mornings.

Breakfast

We'd take it in turns to go to the camp shop in the hope of getting some bread and or croissants or whatever.

We had the gas stove that had come with our kitchen pack so we were able to brew water for tea in a saucepan (French people didn't use to have kettles in those days...)

Unfortunately the warm and otherwise pleasant climate made it difficult on a culinary level because it was impossible to keep things cool for very long. We had a cool box – which is one of those things that you might take with you for an afternoon picnic with a frozen ice pack inside to keep things cool.

But for trying to keep things like milk and butter etc cool for 24 hours a day, 7 days a week, this arrangement wasn't ideal. Admittedly, you could go and exchange your melted ice pack for a fresh one at the camp shop – but that assumed that you could get there while it was open – and that you actually remembered to do it!

The modern me would have a strict routine in place changing over the ice packs at least twice a day but we are, after all, talking about a pair of 17 year old lads who only seemed to remember AFTER they had already been to the shop for the bread, when the butter oozed out of the packet all over the breakfast table.

During breakfast, we had the radio on – don't ask me whose radio it was or where it came from - I just remember that we used to listen to it...

The main commercial pop station in the region at the time was Radio Monte Carlo so we used to have that on all the time. As I recall, the big hits that they played most often were the Ghostbusters theme by Ray Parker Junior and Self Control by Laura Branigan.

On the Beach

After breakfast we would pack our beach things up – towel, bottle of water, sun cream and so on – and head off to the beach for the day.

Needless to say, the beach in August was very busy but not so packed that you couldn't find a place to yourself and not be too close to other people.

There were lots of other English people there, obviously, quite a few Germans and Dutch and a few French as well, although I imagine that any French people in the know would have other places elsewhere along the coast that were not so touristy to go to...

Aside from the obligatory sunbathing and the paddling / swimming in the sea, there are a few other things that stick in my mind about being on this beautiful beach in the South of France.

One was seeing lots of women topless. (nuff said...)

Another was that were were young lads – English mainly, as far as I could tell - who used to walk the length and breadth of the beach all say selling cold drinks. They each had a cool box filled with cans of Coca Cola, Fanta orange, bottles of Perrier water (aimed presumably at the French...) and they would walk along the beach calling out

"Cold Drinks! Boissons Fraiches!"

These drinks cost 10 Francs each - which was a bit expensive as you could buy the self same thing in the grocery shop in town at the edge of the beach for about 2F – but they were at least ice cold and very refreshing and you didn't have to carry them from the shop and try and keep them cool.

I don't know who these lads were – and if they worked in teams or were on their own - or if they were employed by some shady business mastermind behind the scenes. It's the sort of thing that is probably controlled by the Yugoslavian mafia these days but, back then, none of them looked to be being trafficked or overly put upon...

There was also a funny little chap who used to go around the beach all day selling some sort of sweet roasted nuts.

He was definitely French as he didn't dress like a tourist. He wore rather comical long shorts and a sensible shirt and hat to keep the sun off him. He was very heavily tanned and a bit wizened from being in the sun year in year out. I'd guess he was probably 50 or 60 and had probably been selling nuts to the tourists ever since they first started coming to Port Grimaud in the 60s...

He was quite a character and he actually went round and gave one nut to everybody on the beach in the hope that they would like them and buy a packet from him.

He had some special call that he shouted out to let people know he was coming but I was never able to work out what it was he was saying. The modern me would have interviewed him, of course, and found out all about him - but I was very shy and retiring in those days.

I didn't really think the nuts were particularly suitable as beach food, to be honest, but the tactic must have worked otherwise he wouldn't have carried on doing it.

Evening

Then, after a day on the beach, (we didn't just go to the beach every day and stay there all day and do nothing else - by the way, this is just to give you a general idea of our overall timetable...) we would walk back to the campsite, have a shower to get rid the salt and sand and road grit and then have a rest before getting ready to go out in the evening.

The showers were open air cabins (with doors, obviously, just no rooves) round the back of the toilet block. They weren't overly hot but the weather was so warm that it was nice to be able to cool off as well as have a good wash.

On a typical evening we would then walk back into town and go and have a pizza or some other light meal in one of the restaurants. It's funny how when it's hot, you don't want to eat very much – and for me, that is very unusual.

There was also a creêe (French pancake) stand where you could sweet or savoury pancakes with all sorts of different fillings. This was the first time that I'd had a proper French crêpe. They have a special way of doing them, using special flour, so it's not the same if you try and do it yourself at home.

I still enjoy them to this day and always look out for a traditional French crepe stand at the continental markets that you occasionally see touring around the country.

This is a rare photo of me on the holiday to Port Grimaud in 1984. There aren't many pictures of me from this holiday because I took my camera and John didn't – so I took most of the photos.

I also didn't like to take it onto the beach in case it got lost or damaged, so there were fewer photo opportunities overall that were in daylight .

In this picture I am standing with the highly picturesque Port Grimaud marina in the background. Not that you could actually tell from this. I could almost anywhere – the sewage treatment works on the edge of Colne near Boundary Mill, for example, but, no, I am actually at the waterfront in Port Grimaud here.

I am wearing what was known at the time as a "tea bag" t-shirt – so called because they had little holes throughout the material like the perforations in a tea bag. Or, indeed, in an airtex vest. They were quite popular that summer and I'm still waiting for them to come back into fashion so that I can wear mine again, although it seemed to have shrunk in the drawer the last time I tried it on...

Cocktails In The Evening

In the evenings that we went into Port Grimaud, we found a cafe with a nice shaded outside terrace that we liked and made it our regular haunt.

I don't remember what it was called and, looking at maps and photos of the resort on the internet now, I can't really identify where it was or if it is still there - but we certainly liked it at the time.

What was nice about this cafe / bar / restaurant - call it what you will – was that it was on the edge of the square so you could see everything that was going on. They quite often had travelling musicians who came round and played songs for tips so it was a nice way to spend an evening.

We usually sat at the same table so the waiter got to know us over the time that we were there. His name was Christian and we made sure we gave him a good tip every evening so that he looked after us really well.

Aside from the usual beers and cokes and pernods etc , the cafe had an interesting cocktail menu so – being on holiday - we splashed out and tried a few of those. The one I remember enjoying the best and we had that a few times was called a Tamouré – which I can't find mentioned anywhere on the internet so it might just have been an in-house conconction.

As far as I could tell from my own youthful and limited experience of such things, it seemed to be based on brandy and orange and had lots of exciting bits of fruit floating in it, along with the obligatory straws and umbrellas.

We discovered that you could have a large one of these and make it last most of the evening and you'd be less inebriated than if you had spent the same amount of time and more money drinking beer.

American Patrol

On the 14th August – that was the first Tuesday of our stay – there was a big parade in the evening through the town of Port Grimaud of US Navy sailors and a marching band.

It was to commemorate the 40th anniversary of the landing of US troops on the south coast of France as part of Operation Dragoon, following on from the D-Day landings in the north a couple of months earlier.

I suppose they held the parade in the evening because it would be cooler for all the participants. Plus most of the visitors would have been out on the beach during the day!

Mixing With The Other Holidaymakers

The tents in our area were set out in a circle facing into a grassy area with trees all around the back to keep the sun off the tents as much as possible.

There were probably 6 or 8 tents in our cluster and all the holiday makers kept pretty much to themselves.

I am pleased to say that there was no bad behaviour, no late night noise - no drug use and wacky baccy like you'd probably be plagued with now - and it was all very congenial and enjoyable.

In the tent next to us was a chap and his wife / girlfriend who had travelled down on a large motorbike and we had quite few pleasant chats with them over the week they were there.

There was another man / wife couple, across the other side who we nodded hello to from time to time and there was a pair of girls who fascinated us.

They were clearly older than us – probably 20-25 or so – but it's very difficult to guess people's ages from a distance. Having taken a couple of days to work up enough courage, we went over one day and introduced ourselves saying, very chivalrously, that if they "needed any help with anything", all they needed to do was shout.

Looking back now, they came across as sort of trainee teacher types – although I do appreciate that is a grossly unfair generalisation and that not even all trainee teachers probably look like trainee teachers – but you get the idea.

One was called Pam and the other Christine, I think, and it was fairly obvious that they weren't in the least bit interested in we two 17 year old oiks... They'd say hello as they passed by - in a very polite but distanced sort of way - and on the couple of occasions that we casually asked if they would like to go to the bar or some other function, they very politely refused. So there you go. Holiday romance – not.

Manchester Students

On our second week were there, a group of 5 young male students from Manchester took over two of the tents across from where we were staying. They invited us to join them for a few beers one evening and we chatted and got on well together so for a few evenings that week we stayed on the campsite rather than walking all the way into town.

One particular evening, I remember we played a variety of drinking games.

One of them was called Bunnies, where you take it in turns to wiggle your fingers like bunny ears and try and catch out the other players. This game is quite well explained on the internet so I imagine a lot of people already know about it, so I won't further endanger the rain forests – or those squids that provide the ink - by rambling on about it here.

There was another game that was quite memorable. Apart from the name of it – and most of the rules – so, on the off chance that anybody else might recognise what this is supposed to be, here are my recollections of it.

You all sat round the table and everybody had a full bottle of beer each. These were the stubby French 25cl size bottles that they had bought in a big box from the Hypermarché up the road.

A deck of cards was dealt out – one card at a time to each person - and when certain cards came up, the recipient had to drink one or two fingers' level of beer out of their bottle.

There was a lot more to it than that – everybody was given silly names - like "Mr Carrots and Taters" - and you had to refer to them by that name otherwise you were forfeit and had to drink a finger from your own bottle. Then, at certain times in the game, everybody drank a finger at the same time so as not to go thirsty.

There was another occasion - and I don't really remember if this was actually in the same game or a different one (it's all a bit vague, you understand) - where somebody did a "Biggles" and put their fingers round their eyes as if they were wearing aviator's goggles and everybody rushed around outside with their arms outstretched singing the Dambusters theme. It seemed like a good idea at the time, anyway.

Quite whether you won or lost by being the first to empty your bottle of beer, I couldn't really say - but a good time was certainly had by all....

The Swedish Couple

There was another couple who are worth mentioning here.

They weren't staying in our tents and I got the impression they were in one of the swishier villas elsewhere on the site but they occasionally walked through our tent area on the way to the shop or something, I presume.

They were both blond and very well suntanned and I distinctly remember Gary the site rep calling across to them when we had our welcome meeting: "I bet you didn't get THAT suntan in France..."

To which the highly decorative lady threw a coy glance across and mouthed "No..." with a seductive Mona Lisa smile.

I am not exaggerating when I tell you that this couple were both extremely attractive. The lady was beautifully bronzed, had long blond hair and all the right curves in all the right places. The guy was well toned without being overly muscley, looked mature and refined without looking particularly old and had very narrow rimmed glasses on that gave an added look of sophistication.

In short – they looked as if they had stepped right out of a Ryvita advert.

If you had told me then that they were a Swedish airline pilot and his chief stewardess, I could have quite easily have believed you.
But this vision was shattered one day towards the end of our stay at Holiday Marina.

We were sitting around nursing hangovers with some of the Manchester students one morning, drinking tea and coffee without milk, like you do when yours has gone off in your cool box and you can't be bothered to stagger to the shop to get any more... - I think it was probably the last Friday, ie 24th August.

Somebody had left their ghetto blaster on the table outside from the night before so we had it on playing "The Smiths", who were a very popular group at the time.

The Swedish airline pilot was passing – on his own this time – no decorative stewardess - quite possibly in the direction of the ablutions, although I would have thought that the swish villa people would have had their own ablutions.

Anyway, upon hearing the music, he diverted his path and came over to us - and the aloof sophisticated facade that he had carried for the whole of our stay suddenly fell away from his face and was replaced with a broad toothy grin and he said:

"Eeee! Tha've got some grrrrand sounds there, lads..."

He then patted one of us on the shoulder and walked off.

So, not so much Ryvita advert as Boddingtons Bitter!

A Day By The Pool

One day, we decided to forego the delightful walk along the hot dusty busy road all the way into Port Grimaud and stay and laze by the swimming pool on the campsite instead.

It was a nice hot sunny day and, luckily, most of the other campers had decided to go into town or on the beach – or at least somewhere else - as the pool wasn't too busy.

Now, nice as it was to be able to lounge around the pool on a deck chair with a nice cold drink sitting in the sun - as it was the only time I have ever done, it was ok as far as it went.

But, once you've got too hot in the direct sunlight, and had a few swims round to cool off – what do you do then? There's only so much getting sunburnt and swimming it off a guy can stand in a day.

At least on the beach there are different people going by to look at and people sailing, jet skiing and wind surfing in the bay. And people coming round selling things. And women with no tops on. And all sorts of other distractions you don't get around a campsite swimming pool.

So, having enjoyed a morning by the pool, at least, we decided to hike off into Port Grimaud anyway and grab some lunch as swimming does give you one hell of an appetite!

As a dedicated tourist resort, there were plenty of places to try and lots of nice souvenir and gift shops to mooch around.

While we were there – although not necessarily on the same day as the pool experience - I bought myself a t-shirt to take home. It was blue and white horizontal stripes (a bit like the traditional Breton but much narrower lines) and with the "Port Grimaud Cite Lacustre" poisson logo on the front. It's not very clear but I am wearing it in the photo of me taken in Foix in the Pyrenees on my visit there in 1985.

There was a guy on the campsite who sold t-shirts bearing a St Tropez logo so Gids and I bought one of those each as well.

Windsurf Course / Pedalo Ride

One day Gids decided to have a go at windsurfing. There was a sailing school on the beach where you could go and book for an hour and they lent you all the equipment.

I didn't really fancy it so he went on his own and I merely observed from a distance.

I'm glad I didn't try it as all he actually achieved during his hour's tuition was try to stand up on the board, try and lift up his sail, fall over and start again several times – which I didn't think was very much fun.

On another occasion, we tried something much more manageable and that was to hire a pedalo for an hour.

Once we got the hang of peddling at the same time and the nuances of the steering mechanisms, this went pretty well. We decided to head out into the bay for the first half of our hour, then turn round and come back.

It was really nice to be out on the water away from all the other people. It was a gorgeous day with clear blue skies and, although the sun was hot, the little splashes off the sea as we pedalled along served to keep us cool. Once you get a bit further out into the bay, the views of the surroundings were really stunning.

After a few breathers along the way to look at the views, a glance at my watch suggested that it was time to turn around and go back. We did so and saw with a look of horror how far away from the shore we had managed to get!

Obviously, being oblivious to the possibilities of ebbs and tide around the bay, we hadn't really thought of this and, in other circumstances could have found ourselves in a spot of bother. But we put our heads down, pedalled away at a furious pace and eventually got back to the beach where we were able to return the contraption without getting charged any extra.

Boat Trip Around Port Grimaud

Staying with the nautical theme, one afternoon, we decided to hire a boat and coast around the canals of Port Grimaud town. This was a popular pastime and there were several little stands around the marina where they hired very low powered boats for an hour at a time for a reasonable amount.

John actually had his own boat at home and we had taken it out on the River Nene in the past so I let him do the driving while I sat back and pretended to look trendy being seen on a boat at St Tropez bay.

While it may look quaint and old fashioned, the majority of Port Grimaud was only built in the 1960s and they very cleverly constructed it around a series of waterways to make the properties more attractive for tourists.

So, it was a nice afternoon – clear blue skies and sunshine - and we pootled around the waterways of Grimaud in our little boat for an hour. It was a lot warmer on the inland waterways than it was out on the coast with the sea air blowing in, so an hour was about enough for us in the afternoon sun.

The Big Storm

The weather was wonderful for practically the whole duration of our stay at Port Grimaud with hot sun and blue cloudless skies all day and lovely warm summer evenings. Plus – being near the coast and in a tent meant that it wasn't too hot to sleep at night either. Except for the night when we had a massive thunder storm!

As far as I can remember, it was the second Wednesday of our stay which would have been the 22nd August 1984. The day had been perfectly pleasant but we were socialising with the Manchester lads on the campsite when it began to cloud over.

As it was getting dark anyway, we didn't really give much thought to it until spots of rain began to appear.

This caused everybody across the site to rush and move things that had been gaily abandoned all over the place to get them under cover.

We went back to our tent and decided to have an early night – well, an earlier night than usual - after we had braved the showers to get to the ablutions.

It bucketed it down with rain all night and rumbles of thunder announced the arrival of a tropical storm. The storm passed right overhead and there were deafening claps of thunder.

Not being able to sleep, we sat in the doorway of our tent looking at the amazing sight. Lightning illuminated the whole campsite in a way that you normally only see in films and Scooby Doo cartoons.

It was a good job that we were awake, actually, as the rain water started trickling into our tent and we were able to lift things off the floor to protect them.

The storm eventually passed and we tiptoed through the standing water on the floor to get into bed and finally managed to get to sleep.

By the time we woke up, the rain had more or less stopped and the flood water around our camp beds had subsided so we were able to get up and get dressed without getting wet.

Thursday was quite a gloomy day and although the storms didn't return, everything around the campsite was dripping wet.

John had rather sensibly packed all of this dirty clothes into his suitcase ready to take them home but, as his case had ended up standing in water even though we had moved them both right to the back of the tent, it meant that everything in it was damp.

So he had to take everything out of the case, wring the wet things out as best he could and then hang them on a makeshift line that we managed to string up across the tent. We didn't want to hang things outside in case it rained again - but the ambient temperature was quite warm and the things did dry out eventually.

Most of my stuff wasn't in my case so, while I did have to dry out my valise before I could use it, most of the clothes didn't get as wet.

With concerns over whether the storm might return it wasn't a good day to sit out in the open on the beach but once it became clear that it probably wasn't actually going to rain again, we decided to take the motorbikes out to St Tropez. So that was our trip out for Thursday.

Friday started off quite cloudy and chilly but the sun came out eventually and we had a nice day for our last full day in Port Grimaud.

Photos taken around the campsite at Holiday Marina.

Top: Andrew "Fozzie" Foster – one of the Manchester students we met up with during our second week. You get a good view of our tenting area in this shot. & John demonstrating how to use the hired "kitchen pack" properly.

Middle: The other 4 Manchester students. One was called Rick, one was called Lee and I'm afraid I don't remember the other twos' names.

Bottom: John with the two girls from Wales that we met at the Barbecue evening. You can see in the background that they travelled with a different company as their tents were different. Anybody who knows me will realise that I preferred the dark haired older one, obviously... & John getting ready for our motorcycling expedition. In the background you get another view of the tents – plus a better view of the Kitchen Pack....

Up in the Massif des Maures mountains near Le Luc. It's not quite Dennis Hopper in Easy Rider but this is probably the coolest motorcycling photo of me ever taken.

Motorcycling

On the campsite that we were on, they had two motorbikes that you could hire for a day – or half day – and, having originally planned to do a motorcycling tour of northern France, we decided it would be a good idea to take these out for a spin at least once while we were there.

The bikes were a Honda CB125, similar to the one I had at home before I passed my test and moved onto something bigger – and a Honda CM125 which was styled a bit like an American chopper cruiser.

Gids took the CM and I took the CB and we hired them out for a half day to go and check out the mountain scenery to the north of St Tropez Bay.

We didn't go very far as we didn't want to get lost and also didn't want to get stuck too far from civilisation in case we ran into difficulties.

Don't forget – there was no satnav and no mobile phones back in those days so, if you broke down or lost your way, you were pretty much on your own.

We zipped around the warm dry countryside and, as you can see from the photo, the weather was glorious.

We went as far as Le Luc and Draguignan up in the mountains – about 30km or so north of Port Grimaud – but didn't want to go much further as we didn't want to overrun our time with the bike hire.

Had we been a bit better organised, we could have bought a map or a guide book and studied them before we set out. We might then have realised that there were some interesting Abbeys and Monasteries thereabouts to go and have a look at. But when you're 17, on holiday – in 1984 - you don't think about things like that! And we enjoyed what we did – so that was all that mattered.

Motorbikes To St Tropez

We took the bikes out again the week after for an afternoon trek to St Tropez itself – just to be able to say that we had actually been there.

I think it was the Thursday – that would be the 23rd August – because there was a big storm the night before and it rained torrentially for most of the morning. The Booze Cruise was cancelled for that day, not that we had been planning on going on it – but that has just stuck in my memory.

It was only the bad day weather-wise that we had the whole time that we were there, so we couldn't really complain. The sky was heavy and grey, everywhere was soaking wet and, even after the storm, it felt humid and sticky. It looked as if the heavens might open up again at any minute and another storm could easily have been on the cards.

It certainly wasn't a day for going to the beach nor even for the walk into town to look round the shops, so noticing that the motorbikes were available, we made the decision to ride along the road round the bay and have a look at St Tropez, as we were so close and unlikely to ever go there again.

For all the time that we had been there, the coast road around the bay connecting the resorts of St Tropez, Port Grimaud, Ste Maxime and beyond had been chockablock with tourist traffic both ways all day long.

Today was no exception and was probably worse as I imagine that everybody else had the same idea as us. Everywhere was still very wet from the overnight rains. Drops fell from the trees along the side of the road and there was a lot of flooding and surface water lying around.

Because of the poor road conditions and very heavy traffic, we took it very carefully on our hired bikes and it took ages to navigate the 5 or 6 miles to St Tropez.

When we got there, it was impossible to park up anywhere because every single piece of spare concrete and tarmac was occupied by a badly parked car – presumably from a day tripper.

So we rode up and down the main waterfront area for a bit – as far as it was possible with people milling around and getting in the way.

From the very small bit of St Tropez that I saw - ie the obvious tourist haunts and numerous t-shirt shops along the front - I didn't feel that we had missed very much by being in Port Grimaud, instead.

Obviously we didn't know what was where and where the good bits were - and nowhere looks good on cloudy gloomy day – so we never saw the place in its best light, or had time to explore it properly. But at least we had been to St Tropez!

Barbecue Night

On the last night of the holiday at Port Grimaud, we thought we'd treat ourselves and go to the Barbecue Night.

This was held on the campsite in a seated area around the back of the Bullseye, as far as I can remember. I believe they now have a nice restaurant at Holiday Marina. I don't think they did when we were there - and if they did, we certainly never went to it. So this was quite a treat to be able to have hot food without having to cook it ourselves on our under-used kitchen pack and then wash up afterwards – or walk all the way into town for it.

The food was included in the price but the drinks weren't. So this would explain why the barbecue was held close to the bar – to encourage people to go and buy lots of drinks. And, like happens in all the best restaurants, there was a huge delay in getting the food out, just to make sure everybody got plenty of drinks in while they were waiting.

We were seated around big long tables of 10 or 12 and the guests were all from different areas of the campsite – not just our group. The Manchester students didn't go to the Barbecue so we didn't particularly know anybody else there but we entered into the party spirit and chatted to the other people at our end of the table.

There were a couple of girls from Wales sitting near us. I think they might have been called Rachel and Clare, although I might have just made that up – one of those false memories that psychologists talk about in detective dramas. I think they might have been sisters – but more likely cousins as they didn't look anything like each other - and they turned out to be quite chatty and fun.

The food came and went – nice chunky sausages, steaks, potato salad and mixed lettuce leaves, or something of that nature, and then some sort of apple tart for dessert.

Both John and I were being careful not to over indulge with the French beer knowing that we had a busy day of travelling in the morning and had to be up early to finish packing and vacate the tent.

The girls were knocking back the wine and Rachel – we'll stick to calling her Rachel as it's easier, and more chivalrous than saying the "older one" – said that she didn't usually drink very much. A bit later she burped loudly – looked around in great surprise and then announced in a "side of the mouth" confidential manner that she'd just wet herself... She got up from the table saying that she was going to change and I never saw her again. Well, not that night anyway.

The next morning, we trekked halfway across the campsite and managed to find where the girls were staying to check that she / they were all right. Which they were. Rachel seemed to have completely forgotten about the "burping" incident so we didn't mention it either, and she said that she dozed off as soon as she got back to her tent and slept soundly until morning.

I have always wondered. Not desperately and longingly, mind you – just vaguely in passing – whether that might not have been some sort of flirtatious pretext to get me to escort her back to her tent. I assume it was aimed at me, anyway, and not John – the burp certainly came towards me... not that I've spent an awful lot of time studying the efficacity of targeted burping, of course. But who knows...?

As Lucy will tell you, I am extremely obtuse when it comes to nuances in that department. Or any department, if the truth be known. I am a complete nuance–free zone.

We have actually been out at social gatherings and functions together from time to time and she had told me afterwards that some woman there had been slobbering all over me all evening (figuratively speaking only, of course) and I never noticed - so there you go, "Nuances Rn't Us..."

Having said that, once you have been in a swimming pool with 16 bikini-clad Miss Blackpool finalists, it does tend to change your view on Life, the Universe and Everything. 42 doesn't really come into it.

So the fact of the matter is: if you want me to do anything – be it hoovering, ice hockey announcing, or even. indeed, horizontal jogging – there's no point dropping nuances - you need to be a bit more up front about it.

As an interesting Post Script here, I am convinced that I saw the the younger blonde girl (Clare..) appearing on the Blockbusters quiz show on ITV later in the year.

The Flight Home

The journey to Nice Airport on the Saturday was quite interesting. While we had been brought out to our resorts in a luxurious air conditioned coach, we made the return journey in a white mini bus (sort of Ford Transit like...) with all the luggage piled up in the back.

This was, we were told, operated by somebody called "Shuttle Dave" – so called because his name was Dave and he used to shuttle holiday makers to and from the airport.

We had to vacate our tents by 10am and the shuttle wasn't due to leave until 11 or 12 or something like that, so those of us who were going home – there were about 8 of us I think - all congregated in the middle of the campsite with our stuff all piled in a heap.

Once we finally got going, it was quite nice to be in a more artisanal form of transport. The windows were open so we got the rush of fresh air from driving along – but also the varied smells like wind coming in off the sea and the heat of the tarmac all mixed in. It more of an authentic travelling experience than the cocooned air conditioned coach that we had arrived in.

Plus, because we are all crammed in together, we were able to chat to the other passengers – most of whom we hadn't seen before and also the driver and his mate.

There was one hairy moment when I noticed that the back door where the luggage was stored was flapping open and I suggested that the driver pull over and shut it – but, apart from that, it was a pleasant uneventful drive back to Nice Airport.

I was a bit worried about the weight of my luggage at the check in because some of the clothes in my case were still damp from the storm but, luckily, my suitcase came in just under the allowed weight so there was no problem there.

When we took off from Nice, we had the same experience in reverse whereby as the runway sticks out into the ocean as you go haring towards it at high speed you feel as if you are going to end up in the sea. But just at the last minute, the plane lifts and you find yourself soaring above the clear blue waters of the Mediterranean.

One thing I do remember about the flight home was when we were getting off the plane, the piped music being played was "Back In The Old Country" by Tom Robinson.

1987: Italy...? France Actually!

In Summer 1987, I went on a trip to Italy that ended up being a trip to France. Bear with me and all will become clear.

When I was little we had an Italian family living next door to us called Palazzo. The parents were Carmene and Gilda and the children were Serafino (Nino for short) who was a year older than me, and Filomena (Mena) who was a year or so older than him. They went back to live in Caserta in Italy (near Naples) back in 1974 but we kept in touch with Christmas cards over the years.

Fast forward now to 1987 and I had finished studying A Level French and Italian, was a veteran of three trips to the South of France – and I came up with the bright idea of going to visit the Palazzos in Italy.

They had invited us as a family several times in the past so I wrote a letter in my A level Italian saying that it would be nice to go and see them.

I got a telephone call from Nino and we agreed that I would fly over to Naples with my then girlfriend and stay with them for a bit.

We flew on Monarch Air and funnily enough, the weather was better in England when we left than it was when we arrived in Naples. It was overcast and raining but very warm and sticky and the clothes I had on for travelling were much too heavy.

It was very warm all the time we were there so we had to be careful where we went out in the heat of the day.

One day we went to look around the Reggia di Caserta which was a former Royal Palace originally built for the Kings of Naples in the 17th century.

Another day we went to the beach with Nino, Mena and her fiancé Antonio. They were apparently hoping to get married but Mena's dad wouldn't allow it as Antonio didn't have a job. It was fascinating driving through the countryside seeing a different type of agriculture – even from what I had seen in the south of France.

*Above left: Mena,
Nino, Paul & Gary in
the Park in
Peterborough,1974.
Above right: Nino
with Paul on the
balcony at Caserta,
1987*

*Middle left: La Reggia
at Caserta. Middle
right: Paul, Nino,
Antonio and Mena on
the beach at Scauri,
July 1987*

*Bottom left: PB at the
Coliseum in Rome,
July 1987*

At the side of the road, there were people with vans selling huge water melons which you could buy whole or by the slice. There were also lots of fields given over to the cultivation of tobacco.

Rather ironically, the day we went to the beach was the worst weather of the whole time we were there and it was cloudy and muggy all day. Having said that, it would probably have been too hot had the sun been shining.

The food we had was very nice. Gilda worked from home doing dressmaking and mending so she had plenty of time to prepare food every evening. Despite having all the shutters closed for most of the day and everywhere having tiled floors, it was still very hot in the apartment and she used to change clothes 3 or 4 times a day for "hygiene" purposes.

It was quite common for people to go out walking late in the evening when it turned cooler, and this explains why people in hot countries tend to take siestas in the middle of the day.

One evening when it was cooler, we went to a bar with Nino and some of his friends and had a few Italian beers. It was just after the local big club Napoli had won the Italian football championship for the first time ever - under Diego Maradona - so everybody was still talking about that.

Towards the end of the week, some sort of calamity occurred within the Palazzo household. Somebody had been taken ill somewhere – some cousin or aunt or somebody in Pescara some 200km away on the other side of the country – and Gilda had to rush to go and look after them, apparently. Because of this we wouldn't be able to stay as long as we had planned and had to make alternative arrangements for the rest of our time away.

We were actually going to go to Rome for a few days anyway so had some of our stuff packed but we had to come up with a new idea as to what to do afterwards.

We took the train to Rome and the journey was not unpleasant. It was sunny outside and quite warm on the train even with the windows open.

We went right past Monte Cassino and it is a really impressive site, with the ancient abbey high up on a steep mountain top, 520m / 1710 ft above sea level. A quick glance is enough to explain why it was so difficult to take in battle during WW2.

It was only about an hour and a half to Rome and we arrived there early afternoon.

On the station platform there were a load of unofficial porters and one asked if we wanted an hotel and grabbed our cases and walked off with them.

We followed him to a hotel not too far from Roma Termini station which was just down a side street and quite pleasant looking. He plonked our cases down and I paid him whatever it was he asked for - 5000 lire or whatever.

Our first thought was to decide what to do next as our return flight was not booked for another week and, with it being a cheap charter flight, there was no way of changing it.

Judith suggested that we might be able to go and visit her French penfriend in La Rochelle as she and her family had been over there in July 1985 and had been invited to go back any time. I know people always say "come back anytime" but whether they really mean it or not, who knows…

We spent a ridiculous amount of money using the hotel phone to ring Judith's mum in England to get the phone number for the Girard family in La Rochelle and then another ridiculous amount of money to call Valerie to find out if we could go and visit them.

Luckily, the Girards were at home - and had no immediate plans - so it was agreed that we could go and visit them for a few days after we had been around Rome rather than cutting our holiday short.

As it had been quite an eventful day, we decided to stay close to the hotel for something to eat and then prepare for a day of sightseeing on the morrow.

The change in plan had upset me and I didn't really enjoy the day that we spent looking around Roma. We went to the coliseum as that was very well signposted and easy to find.

The next morning we went to Roma Termini station with our luggage ready to catch the train. It was quite a pleasant journey. The sun was shining and the sky was blue but the train was quite airy and not overly full. On the way north, the train followed the coast so we saw lots of interesting places and beautiful beaches through the windows.

We went past Pisa and saw the famous leaning tower through the train window and survived on snacks that we bought off the sellers who congregated on the various platforms at every town that the train stopped. After a 12 hour journey of 700km, we ended up in the early evening at Ventimiglia (which I have mentioned before).

There was a bit of confusion as to whether we needed to change trains or if they were going to carry out the passport formalities on the train and transport the carriages on into France.

After talking to about three different railway staff at Ventimiglia, I discovered that we had to take all of our luggage off the train, go through a passport and customs post and then get onto another train on the French side. Having wasted a half an hour or so through having to make enquiries, this ended up being a rush to get to the other train before it left.

However, when we did get on the French train, there was hardly anybody on it and we had a whole compartment of 8 seats to ourselves. After a couple of stops heading into France, two German lads came into our compartment so we had to budge up a bit but we still had two seats each to spread out on.

We travelled through Menton, Monaco, Nice, Cannes, Frejus, Aix en Provence, Nimes, Montpellier, Beziers, Narbonne, Carcassone and Toulouse – the sort of journey which under other, less rushed, circumstances I would love to do again. Over the course of the journey along the south coast of France, the train gradually filled up and there were no seats left anywhere on the train.

It was rather uncomfortable to be sitting up all night on a stuffy train compartment full of other people and I just kept sipping on bottled water to keep hydrated and try to keep cool. Early on in the morning I discovered from talking to some fellow passengers that the train we were on was heading to Biarritz – which, again, I would have liked to have gone to under other circumstances – and I found out that we needed to change at Toulouse to get the train to Bordeaux.

So, after another 14 or so hours and 620km on the train, we finally got off at Toulouse, grabbed a little breakfast at the station and then leapt onto the connection for Bordeaux.

At that time of the morning, the Bordeaux train was quite empty so there was plenty of room to spread out and rest up after having had a rather disrupted night. 2.5 hours and 250km later we arrived at Bordeaux St Jean station where we had a bit of a wait until the train to La Rochelle.

We eventually arrived in La Rochelle in the early afternoon and were picked up by the Girard family and taken to their home where we were fed and went and had a long rest until tea time.

The Girards lived in a village called Marans just outside La Rochelle itself. Here was Valerie, the daughter, her younger brother Didier, mother Madeleine and father Yves. There was also an older brother who was away doing army service who I didn't meet.

The father Yves went out to work every day – I never found out what he did and where – but he also had a large amount of land around his house and his own cottage farming industry.

In the yard they had a huge trapdoor and it opened to a wide deep staircase that led underground. Here they had their own underground cellar – about 3m x 3m - with shelves all round full of jars of preserves – jams, pickles etc plus bottles and bottles of wine and more bottles of what they called "Eau de vie", which was homemade hooch made from their own produce.

Madeleine was a superb cook and we had very good meals all the time we were there. In view of the fact that we had turned up with very little notice, they did very well to accommodate us and were the perfect hosts.

149

Photo left: Bar evening in Caserta – PB, Nino & 2 of his friends.

Photos below:

The Leaning Tower of Pisa (circled) viewed from the train window.

On the train from Toulouse to La Rochelle

PB at Bordeaux Station and The harbour at La Rochelle.

Photos top: The agricultural land behind the Girard family's farm house. Sylvie, Didier, Yves & Madeleine.

Photos above: PB with Valerie and Sylvie. PB on the Calais to Dover ferry at 3am.

Madeleine's sister – the Body family - also lived in Marans next to the river (Sevre Niortaise) and they had a daughter called Sylvie who was older than Valerie and was a school teacher. Most of the time during the day we went out with Valerie and Sylvie who showed us things of interest in the local area. We went into La Rochelle itself one afternoon for a look round.

Once we arrived in Marans, I called my mum and told her that we were stuck for money and couldn't get home. As luck would have it, her boss who she worked for on Peterborough market at the time happened to have £300 cash on him the next day as he had sold a trailer and he let my mum borrow it to send to us. She took it to the bank in town and they arranged to have it transferred to us in France. We had to go to a particular branch of Credit Agricole in La Rochelle, show our passports and we were able to take out the money in French Francs.

So, a week or so after we arrived in Marans, we took the train and headed for Paris on the way home.

It was a 4 to 5 hour journey on the train to Paris and we went through places I had never been to before. We went through Niort, Poitiers, Tours and Orleans and then took the Metro from Paris St Lazare to the Gare du Nord to catch the boat train.

There was a big hoo-ha going on at the Gare du Nord when we got there. The platforms were full of people milling around with luggage piled all over the place - and the arrival and departure boards didn't have anything on them.

I never actually discovered what was going on but we somehow managed to get two seats on a train to Calais without having to hang around for too long. There was as much fuss going on at Calais as there was in Paris but we ended up on a ferry that sailed in the middle of the night and docked at Dover early the next morning.

Once we got onto the train from Dover to London, things calmed down a bit and the rest of the journey home to Peterborough passed without incident.

And so ended a fascinating, if rather exhausting, journey that took us some 3089 Km right across Europe from Caserta in the south of Italy back to Peterborough via the Cote D'Azur and La Rochelle.

Journey	Time (hrs)	Km
Napoli to Roma	1.5	220
Roma to Ventimiglia	12	700
Ventimiglia to Toulouse	14	620
Toulouse to Bordeaux	2.5	250
Bordeaux to La Rochelle	3	185
La Rochelle to Paris	4	470
Paris to Calais	3	300
Calais to Dover	1.5	80
Dover to London	1.75	128
London to Peterborough	1	136
Totals:	47.25	3089

1987/88:
A French Connection

Marie-Laure Sansom, 1988

I started working at Baker Perkins - as it was still known back then - in July 1985 in the admin office of the PMC fitting shop, which I enjoyed very much.

After I had been there for a year, my manager Roger Smith asked me if I would like to do a day release course at the Peterborough Technical College – to help with my general personal development.

This wasn't part of my job or anything to do with a formal career path, it was just something that he wanted to do for me – which I thought was very good of him.

I gratefully accepted and went on to sign up for a BTEC HNC in Business & Finance, which was held on Wednesdays and ran for two years from September 1986 to June 1988.

According to whatuni.com, *"A Higher National Certificate (HNC) is a level 4 vocational qualification that takes one year to complete full-time, or two years part-time. An HNC is equivalent to the first year at university. You can generally enter a bachelor's degree at year 2 once you complete an HNC."*

Now, this was a really interesting course and I thoroughly enjoyed doing it - and not just because I got to have a day off work in the middle of the week! I got to meet a load of interesting people from other companies around Peterborough - like Thomas Cooks – and the course content was very useful.

Over the 2 years, we did study modules in a range of different topics, such as Economics, Accounting, Statistics, Report Writing, Employee Relations, Interviewing, Law...

And we even did a computer module learning how to use Databases and Spreadsheets – which are commonplace now but most people had never even heard of them at the time.

However, one thing that we didn't cover was languages and that was a bit of a concern for me. My eventual ambition was to work with languages for my main job – either at Baker Perkins or elsewhere - and I was worried that, by no longer being regularly exposed to them, any fluency that I had acquired in French and Italian might begin to suffer as a result.

I didn't really want to start any evening classes as my BTEC course ran on until 7pm on a Wednesday – and, as I started work at 7.30 am in the mornings, I didn't want to be out late on other evenings as well.

I wrote a letter to my former French teacher at school, Mrs Roberts, and asked her if she could put me in touch with anybody who could help me out with a bit of French and Italian conversation for an hour a week just to keep me in the habit.

She very kindly gave me the phone numbers of the French and Italian language assistants who were working for the year at Stanground School and said they'd be happy to meet up with me to discuss arrangements. These were university students who had come to England for their year abroad in the same way as English students who are studying French go and spend a year in a French speaking country.

So on different days, I met up with Marie Laure (French) and Gabriella (Italian) for coffee in town and they both agreed to give me an hour's conversation once a week for £5 a go.

As I finished work at 4pm, we were able to have our sessions straight after they had finished at school so it worked well for all of us. And that kept me going for the year.

By 1988, I had finished my BTEC course and was working in the commercial department of Baker Perkins. I then had access to the in-house language courses that they were running and over time was able to do regular classes and take City & Guilds exams in French, Italian, German and Spanish.

Above left: St Etienne on the map of France (Source: www.ontheworldmap.com)
Above right: A Baker Perkins G14 printing press not unlike the one that was being installed at IGPM in 1988 (Source: www.pressxchange.com)

1988: St Etienne

In the spring of 1988 I travelled abroad for work for the first time. I was only 20 years old at the time, so this was quite a big undertaking for me to embark upon.

My company - Baker Perkins PMC (or APV Baker PMC as it had become known by then after an unfortunate corporate merger) had sold and was installing a magazine printing press at IGPM in St Etienne. IGPM stood for Impression Graphique Presse et Magazine and, according to my internet research, the company is not actually operating any more, which if that is true - is a shame.

When I went there in 1988, they were opening a new building up in the Rue de la Robotique on an industrial park close to the centre of St Etienne. The building had been constructed especially to install our machine in and the offices and other areas were still just a shell waiting to be finished off.

Apparently, the South Of France technically starts at Valence on the 45th Parallel, which is pretty much on a level with Bordeaux, Turin, Venice and Zagreb.

St Etienne is 100km north of Valence, 60km south of Lyon, and therefore just outside the start of the Midi.

But all the same, it is 800km from Calais and only 300km from Montpellier so it is certainly more south than north and the weather was pleasantly warm – without being over hot - all the time that I was there.

Just to give you a little bit of background here, I was working in the Commercial department at Baker Perkins. Baker Perkins originally produced biscuit making machinery and bread machines for large commercial bakeries but over time they diversified and in the 1960s started making printing presses as well. In 1985, they were divided into three separate companies and PMC was the Printing Machinery Company.

I won't go into what I normally did at work at this point. That's probably worth a separate book on its own and the French travel aspect is what is relevant to this particular volume, so we'll stick to that for the time being.

In brief, the project coordinator who had been overseeing the press installation since it had begun several months earlier, Steve Lee, had to come back to England for a bit and he was the main French speaker on the installation site.

As I was the office French expert at that time, I was asked if I would mind going over there for a week to help with communications with the customer and local suppliers and tradesmen while he was away.

I readily agreed and, a few days later, found myself being driven down to Heathrow Airport with David Greenhalgh who was a senior engineer on the Field Engineering Department (FED) and Graham Perkins who was a printer employed on our installation staff and was just grabbing a lift to the airport on the way to a different customer.

We flew from Heathrow to Lyons and, due to a shortage of seats on the British Airways flight, we flew Club Class – which was quite a treat.

On the plane David recognised a chap called Alan Smith who was a commissioning engineer with the company Harland Simon - who supplied the drive motors for our presses and it turned out that he was going to IGPM as well.

Alan was going to be stopping in the same hotel as us and, as he had a hire car booked, we met up with him after the baggage reclaim and passport control and we all set off together.

After a lot of getting lost in the dark, we eventually found our way to the Novotel hotel that we had all been booked in to and went to check in and find the other BP personnel.

They were all in the bar so we had a freshen up and a bite to eat in the hotel restaurant - French Novotels always have very good food by the way – and then caught up with the others.

The rest of the team at that time consisted of Greg Maxwell who was the printer who was going to oversee the start up of the press, Clive Wardle who was the electronics engineer in charge of the controls, Ken Dixon who was overseeing the installation of the electrical cables, and Mark Leaning who was handling the finish of the mechanical installation.

The guys were a little surprised to see me - because office people didn't tend to go out on installations - but at the same time they were pleased as they had already been having communication difficulties since Steve Lee had departed.

Also in the bar was a German engineer from, I think, VITS or TEC Systems - who were supplying the hot air dryer for the press. Apart from the Baker Perkins equipment, a printing press also comprises numerous other major components and the suppliers of those bigger items would normally send their own people to commission them.

This won't mean much to anybody else but the press being installed was a Baker Perkins G14 with a C1 (single chopper) folder.

I won't explain the process of installing a printing press just now – although it is fascinating. That would be better done later on when I tell you about my time at the installation at Sima Torcy from October 1988 to March 1989. I was there right from the start of that one and will be able to cover it in a much more logical sequence then.

Suffice to say that the machine was more or less in place and ready to be started up, which is why the drive motor guy had been called in.

Working on an installation on site is not a 9 to 5 job. If something needs finishing, you stop later – or go in early, or miss lunch – or work weekends - and although I was technically office staff, I was there to help the guys out. So I had to be with them all the time and go where they went.

These were the same engineers who, if they were on call in the office at home, would have to rush out to work on a breakdown so they were used to working long days and odd hours whereas I wasn't.

I immediately became the one who had to translate all the menus and specials boards at the restaurants that we went to and also help out with any other communication issues that arose.

Away from the actual installation site, some of the more unusual things I had to help with included:

- Going with Clive to the St Etienne branch of the car rental company to get his faulty hire car replaced and arrange for the new one to be handed back at the branch at Lyon Satolas airport when we were due to leave.

- Going with one of the AL Electrics engineers to report to the police that his car had been broken into

- & helping Greg complain to the hotel management that their laundry department had shrunk a pair of very expensive trousers...

One of the first jobs that I was involved with at the installation in the factory was helping Greg to set up the dampening recirculation system.

This is an important part of the printing process – at least it was back then, they may use a different technique now, what with all the developments in technology – and what the dampening did was help wash off any excess ink from the printing plate so that only the required image would transfer onto the paper.

This was done by applying a mixture of water, alcohol and special dampening solution (sometimes called etch) across the plates while the machine was in operation.

The mixture had to be exactly calculated and a special machine was used to ensure that the correct amount of each substance was used in the mix. This system pumped the dampening solution into the print units and drained off the used product to be reused until it was no longer suitable.

And the use of this process explains why litho print works always have a strong smell of alcohol hanging around them.

That is just one example and I basically did lots of other little "helping out" jobs around the press installation – holding a spanner, or calling out when a particular light went on or off – and general interpreting when dealing with the customer's staff, deliveries and other ad-hoc eventualities.

With Steve Lee not due back anytime soon, it became apparent that I wasn't only going to be there for a week after all. It ended up as three in the end, which I can't say bothered me in the slightest. How can anybody complain about being in the South Of France and getting paid for it..?

Day Trip To Switzerland

Nothing much was due to happen at the weekend so Greg announced that, on the Sunday, he was going to drive to Switzerland for the day. This was perfectly do-able as Geneva was just 200km from St Etienne - and I was determined not to miss out - so he, Clive and I had a good breakfast at the hotel and made an early start.

It was a very pleasant drive through the Massif Central and Savoie mountain scenery and I was interested to see some of the names of the places that we drove by:

Bourg en Bresse – famous for its blue cheese

Chambery – famous ski resort and previously the seat of the Kings of Savoy

Aix les Bains – famous spa town

Annecy – lakeside ski resort and home town to French student Marie-Laure Sansom - who I used to have conversation lessons with back in Peterborough a year or so before.

The day was bright and dry but not overly sunny – which was much better for driving - and we made good time in getting to Geneva.

It was really exciting arriving in Switzerland for the first time and seeing the famous lake.

But I have to say that my overall impressions on this brief visit were that the place was clean, cold (it was only mid March after all...) and, above all, it was CLOSED...!

Yes it was Sunday lunchtime and everything was closed in Switzerland!

Even the famous fountain wasn't working - which was a great disappointment to me as I had been really looking forward to seeing it, having remembered it from the opening credits of The Champions TV series from the 1960s.

Greg was annoyed as he had wanted to buy a cuckoo clock and some Swiss chocolate for his children so we looked at the map for somewhere else interesting to go to for the rest of the day.

We briefly toyed with the idea of going through the Mont Blanc tunnel and into Italy but thought that was pushing it a bit for a day trip – with work the next day, so instead we settled for Chamonix which was 80km south of Geneva back over the French border.

Chamonix is a famous ski resort, high up in the Alps and at the base of Mont Blanc, France's highest mountain. With it being in the middle of the Alpine ski-ing season, everywhere was covered in snow when we got there.

There were people walking around in ski wear and carrying skis on their shoulders and there were horses and carriages with skids instead of wheels and the delightful jingling of bells that they had slung around their halters. It was just like a scene out of a James Bond film.

By the time we had parked the car and started walking into town, it had started snowing – nothing heavy, just delightful light flakes of snow to add to the charming atmosphere!

Although I have done lots of interesting things over the years, I have never been on a ski-ing trip - so that is the closest I have been and it is still a wonderful memory over 30 odd years on.

I hadn't taken a camera with me to St Etienne. Back then people didn't carry cameras around in their pockets all the time as they were bulky to carry, easy to damage and expensive to repair or replace.

Plus, don't forget that I had originally signed up for spending a week in a factory – and not gadding around half of Europe, as my mum might call it...!

It turned out that Greg did actually have a small camera with him and he took a photo of Clive and me with the light snowfall drifting down around us and Chamonix in the background. I don't know if the photo actually came out or not - and I never saw it if it did, which is a shame as it would have been a nice memento.

I am pretty sure that we must have had something to eat when we got to Chamonix but, for the life of me, I can't remember where we went or what we had. That is quite unusual for me as my memory for trivia is quite good usually – especially in the gourmand department.

I do remember that we went round a few souvenir shops so that Greg could look at cuckoo clocks and I bought an ornament to put on the mantelpiece at home.

We didn't stay very long in Chamonix as the prospect of a long drive back in the dark wasn't very appealing so we headed off taking more or less the same route that we had come by.

So that is the story of my one and only ever visit to Switzerland – oh, and Chamonix.

All courtesy of Steve Lee's home absence – and his car, on which we added 560Km on the clock!

Football – Or Not...

The second weekend that I was in St Etienne some of us had planned to go and watch a football match as St Etienne were - and still are - a famous French team. The guys told me that when Monaco had come to play them shortly before, the team which at that time included England star Glenn Hoddle, had stayed in their hotel!

Unfortunately, I was taken ill on the Friday night, having eaten something that didn't agree with me and was laid up in my hotel room all weekend.

Without me to help with communications, the guys decided they didn't want to go to the football match, which was a bit of a shame, and I was gutted as well to have missed out on this once in a lifetime opportunity to go and watch St Etienne play.

Dining Out

While we often stayed in the hotel for dinner in the evening, it was always nice to go out somewhere else for a change as well.

The lads had already been in St Etienne for several months on the installation so they had already had a chance to go round and suss out some good places to eat.

There was a bakery cum cafe near to the industrial estate that we were working on so we usually walked there to get baguettes and sandwiches at lunchtime but in the evening, it was nice to have a proper meal.

There are two nice places that I remember going to on several occasions.

I'm afraid I can't really remember where they were as I didn't drive at the time and you never take as much notice of landmarks if you are not having to navigate for yourself.

The first one was in the centre of St Etienne. I think it might have been on or near the Place Jean Jaures – or if not, we may have just parked there to get there.

I don't remember what it was called but it was a cafe restaurant that was run by an English chap – so that was a nice Oasis of English conversation in the middle of French France!

The other was a restaurant in a village just on the outskirts of the town and this was very typically French and used lots of local produce.

I remember that Greg Maxwell loved the trout dish that they had there and that he ordered that every time we went. It came with those tiny little roast potatoes that you can get everywhere now but I had never seen them in those days and thought they were wonderful.

I was not a big fish eater in those days and I always stuck to a meat dish to ensure that my healthy appetite was sustained. I did have a taste of Greg's "truite", however, and can confirm that it really was delicious.

Le Top 50

After a day's work at the installation site, we normally went back to the hotel and had a bath / shower and a bit of a rest before meeting up in the restaurant to have dinner.

This time of the day normally coincided with a French music programme called Top 50 (Top Cinquante) that was broadcast on Canal + every weekday. This was a good programme to have on in the background while you were having a bath or rest or whatever as it was mainly music and didn't need a whole lot of effort to be able to follow, even if your French wasn't very good.

I would say that my interest in French music and French singers comes from this point – although I did already like Jeanne Mas and her "Johnny Johnny" song that I'd heard when I was in Montpellier in 1985 and bought the single back then.

Canal + was actually a subscription channel and showed mainly films that were encrypted.

But at certain times of the day, it showed programmes without encryption so that you could watch them normally (without screwing your eyes up...) and the Top 50 was one of those.

It was presented by a very photogenic chap called Marc Toesca and he had quite a following among teenyboppers at the time.

Obviously, with having to fill a full hour's programme every day, they played a wide variety of music from the French charts – not just the top songs all the time – so it was a good way of getting to hear lots of different music.

That said, the number one single in France all the time that I was there on that visit was the rather mushy "Nothing's Gonna Change My Love For You" by Glenn Madeiros (8 weeks in total - 12th March to 7th May), which got a bit boring after you had heard it a couple of times.

However, some French songs / artists that I did discover and like during this period included:

"Boys and Girls" by Charlie Makes the Cook

"Vélomoteur" by Les Calamites

& "Du Rhum Des Femmes" by Soldat Louis

(check them out – they are all available on YouTube these days...)

One day towards the end of my stay in St Etienne, one of the French printers who we were training said that he was going to the Hypermarché at lunchtime, if anybody wanted anything.

I immediately chirped up that I would like a lift - as the opportunity of poking around a French Hypermarket for an hour was one I couldn't resist, so he kindly took me with him. Don't forget that, back in 1988 I didn't have a driving licence - nor a car - so I had to rely on being driven around by other people. I had a motorbike at home on which I had passed my test in 1985 but didn't pass my car test until August 1990.

So I made the most of the trip to the Hypermarché (which was huge and sold everything...) and bought some supplies for the lads and I also splashed out on a few French records for me to take home.

I bought the 7" singles of "Boys and Girls" and "Vélomoteur", the recently released "Jeannea Mas En Concert" Live double album and the new "Première Bordée" album by Soldat Louis - who were like a French version of the The Pogues and the Men They Couldn't Hang, who were two bands that I was very much into at the time - and still am, in fact.

Press Start Up

In the last week of my stay in St Etienne, things got really exciting as the printing press was ready to start up.

Everything had all been connected together and all the constituent parts tested mechanically and electrically individually - and it was now time to set the machine running as a complete press.

We'd already had the IGPM print crew who were going to be operating the machine training with us for a week on setting things up and they would now be running the press under Greg Maxwell's guidance and learning how to manage the various settings and adjustments that would need doing.

All of the equipment had been thoroughly tested back at the factory before it was shipped out to France. The printing units were run individually - without ink or paper - for a certain number of hours at different speeds to check they were all OK and the folder was also rigorously tested running plain paper through it on all the different fold settings.

I had seen this done many times before when I worked in the admin office for the PMC fitting shop – from July 1985 to November 1987 - which was where the print units and folders were assembled and later tested.

Having had no engineering training myself – and being crap at anything practical - I always found it fascinating to see how these huge machines started off as a basic set of heavy metal side frames and over a period of time had all the innards installed to finish up with a high precision technological working piece of equipment.

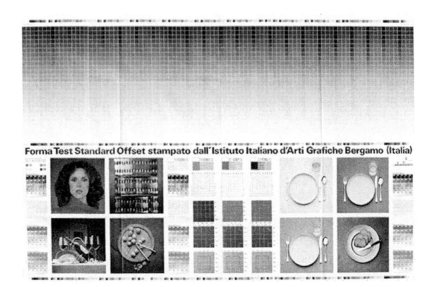

Example of an early model Brunner test plate image. Skin tones and food colours are the most difficult to reproduce authentically in printing. This image looks better and makes more sense in colour, obviously... (Source: www.systembrunner.com)

Everybody in the company was greatly proud of the machinery that we produced and there was always a special sense of achievement when you saw them being tested ready for despatch to the customer.

Here again with the site installation, everything had to be tested mechanically together first – ie reelstands, print units, hot air dryer, chill rollers, folder, main drive etc at different speeds to a particular test schedule and this was then repeated running plain paper through the machine.

Eventually, once all that had been satisfactorily completed, the ink tests were able to commence.

Printing quality at that time was – and I believe still is - usually assessed by running a test plate which had particular characteristics to be able to gauge colour quality, image clarity and various other technical things.

One company that was very well respected in this area was Brunner in Switzerland and we often used their Eurostandard test plates for this purpose.

In fact, it was often set out in the terms of the Contract of Sale that the press be certified to be operating within the norms of a Brunner test before it could be signed off and certain payments released.

As it turned out, they didn't run a Brunner test at IGPM - at least not while I was there, anyway. What they used for their initial print tests and machine fine-tuning was a low quality commercial brochure for a French supermarket chain – the sort of thing that you regularly get inside local papers these days with the week's special offers at Iceland or Lidl or TJ Hughes...

When I say "low quality" here, by the way, that's not a derogatory comment on the customer or the importance of the print job.

It's purely a printing term referring the fact that the job was done on a low weight paper stock with very little silicone coating applied – and quite the other end of the scale from, say, the high quality Vogue fashion magazine, which was printed on much heavier paper stock with considerably more silicone applied to make it more glossy to the feel.

The Italian edition of Vogue was printed on a Baker Perkins G16 press at Amilcare Pizzi in Milan, by the way, and - as another example - the Mail on Sunday's You magazine used to be printed on a G16 at Chantry Web in Wakefield.

Even though this first IGPM job was "only" give-away advertising leaflets for a budget supermarket, the actual colour images still had to be clear and crisp to make the items featured look desirable.

So, the press was up and running and the printers were dashing about doing their thing adjusting here, twiddling there, and so on.

Because the rest of the building was still empty and the finishing line equipment wasn't going to be installed until after the Easter break, the printed copies were all spilling off the folder delivery onto the floor in a big heap.

Normally you would have a series of conveyors to take the finished copies away heading into stacker where they would be bundled together and then taken off to be trimmed, if they were finished leaflets, or taken to a bindery to be combined with other printed sections and maybe a cover if it was for a bigger magazine.

Anyway, none of that was installed and the copies were piling up on the floor around the exit of the folder.

When running at full capacity, the C1 folder could produce 45.000 copies an hour so you can see how quickly the mound of paper would build up.

Everybody else was busy looking at things around the press – the IGPM printers, Greg, our engineers – while I was just standing around like a spare tool watching.

So I decided to make myself useful and gathered up all the copies off the floor and dumped them in a big skip that had been brought in for the purpose of removing the paper waste.

I then positioned myself crouched down and caught the copies as they came off the folder conveyor and took them straight to the skip – which was fun for a few minutes, until my back began to ache.

Just as I feared I might have to wimp out and give up, Greg came over and put his arm round my shoulder.

He said in a very reassuring manner:

"Come on mate, you're not paid to do that..." and he guided me off towards our portakabin, adding "Let's go and make some tea..."

On the last day that we were there before coming home for the Easter break, some sales people from a French ink supplier called Lorilleux came to visit IGPM.

Whether they were already their ink supplier and had just come to look over the new printing press, or whether they were hoping to get the contract to supply ink for the new machine, I am not too sure.

The main thing that I remember learning from their visit was that the French term for a printing problem known as ink fly or misting was "la voltige".

Ever keen to keep in with everybody, the sales guys took Greg, Clive and I out to lunch at a nice restaurant where we had a great meal and lots of wine.

Luckily there wasn't much to do in the afternoon as they were cleaning down the press ready for the Easter shut down so we went back to the hotel for a snooze and to get packed ready to leave the next day.

Flying Out From Lyon

Our flight from Lyons airport was very early the next morning. I seem to think that it was so early that the full breakfast wasn't yet available at the hotel so we had to make do with coffee and rolls.

Any nibbles and drinks that I couldn't fit into my luggage I left outside Mark Leaning's bedroom as he was going to stay on and do odd jobs during the quiet period.

I drove with Clive so that I could help him take his replacement hire car back to the depot and do any explaining that might have been needed, while Greg travelled with Alan in his hire car.

It was 75 Km to Lyon airport but luckily that early in the morning there was very little traffic on the roads.

Back then it still had its original name of Lyon Satolas which was taken from the village of Satolas-et-Bonce near where it was built – rather like Paris Charles de Gaulle airport is also known as Roissy for the same reason.

However in 2000, the airport was renamed Lyon-Saint Exupéry Airport in honour of the Lyon born aviation pioneer and writer Antoine de Saint-Exupéry, on the centenary of his birth.

You can imagine how early it must have been because, even after we had dealt with the hire cars, gone through the check in and got to the departure lounge, it was still pitch black outside!

In the departure lounge we happened upon Mr Mike Smith who was the chairman of the Baker Perkins group – the very top boss, who I had never met before.

Greg – who, himself, only knew Mr Smith from photos - went over and introduced himself and us and we had a few minutes politely chatting about where we had all been to be in Lyons at the crack of dawn.

Mr Smith introduced his travel companion as Mark Gibbard – Group Personnel. They both looked very smart and fresh considering the early hour of the morning, with their suits and ties and very smooth and executive with their suit carriers over their shoulders.

Greg was also very smart with his travelling blazer and tie on but I'm afraid that I rather let the side down as I was wearing several layers of clothes that I couldn't fit into my luggage and the combination of that and feeling like shit at having to get up so early – and not having had time to have a shower - probably left me looking rather sweaty and uncomfortable.

It turned out that Mr Smith's party had been visiting an engineering company called Pavailler in Valence which was then a part of the Baker Perkins group making bakery equipment - and is still in fact, going strong today.

Luckily, as we were flying business class, we had a decent breakfast on the plane and arrived at London Heathrow a bit more refreshed.

Alan Smith was going back to Port Sunlight on the Wirral where he lived and Greg and Clive were going to zip back to Peterborough and report in at the office on the way home.

The last thing I wanted to do on a Friday afternoon after such an early start was show my face at the office, knowing that there would be 3 weeks' worth of paperwork waiting for me to go through, so I said that I would take the train, thank you very much, and we all went our separate ways.

Different hair – same trip! Photo left: PB on top of the Arc de Triomphe in July 1988. The Sacre Coeur can be seen far away in the background. I still have that Cramps t-shirt! Photo right: PB with Parisien backdrop and the Eiffel Tower in the distance.

Summer 1988: Paris

In the summer of 1988 I went for a brief holiday to Paris.

Now, this may sound a bit odd to anybody who has shown the stamina and fortitude – and extreme patience – required to have got thus far into this book with me, and enjoyed reading the minute details that I have gone into with regard to lots of trivial, yet interesting, things - but I really have very little recollection of this particular trip.

To make things easier on all of us, let's start off with what I DON'T remember – and then move on to the things that I do.

For a start, I don't actually remember how we got there. I think we might have flown because it was only a 3 or 4 day City break and to spend a whole day taking the train and ferry there and doing the same thing coming back again would have been a huge waste of "Paris- time".

I would certainly have thought that if I / we had spent an hour on the train down to London, another hour or so on the Underground carting cases around, 2 hours on the train to Dover, more carting of cases around at the port, an hour on the ferry – probably feeling sick –

carting cases at Calais, and then a 3 hour train journey to the French capital, I would probably have remembered it. Especially if I then did the self-same thing in reverse a few days later.

So I probably didn't do that in July 1988 on this city break to Paris. I must have flown (in a plane, obviously) but can't say that I actually remember that either. So it's all a bit of a mystery!

The first thing that I do remember about this visit to Paris is sitting in a taxi driving though the streets of the romantic city on a sunny late afternoon / early evening and seeing some memorable sights (which I no longer remember...) plus the odd welcoming glimpse of the Eiffel Tower in the background between the other buildings.

Having really only ever crossed Paris by the Metro before - and only ever having spent a half day "on the surface" there when I was 12, a couple of hours with Mrs Roberts in 1984 and a night on a hard station floor in 1985, my geographical knowledge of what was actually where in the city was rather sketchy.

As such, I was a bit concerned that the taxi driver might be taking us for a ride – both literally and metaphorically – and taking a rather circuitous route to our hotel.

I fully appreciate that, with bags and cases and looking obviously English - and asking to be taken to a tourist hotel, we clearly looked like visitors / tourists but I was trying at least to come across as a seasoned traveller and Paris-connoisseur as far as the taxi driver was concerned.

Unfortunately, this attempt at sophisticated cosmopolitanism was brutally scuppered when my travelling companion suddenly pointed out of the window and delightedly squealed out in the worst fen accent you could possibly imagine:

" Oh loo-ook! Is that the Eiffel Towaarrrr? Oh wo-ow...!"

Anyway, we must have finally got to the hotel, because I do remember being there.

I don't remember what it was called but it was one of those hotels that was just a doorway leading off from the street, with shops beneath it and the reception and rooms on the upper floors.

It was clean and comfortable and the only downside was that we didn't have a shower in our room and had to use one along the hall. On top of that, you could only use it at certain times of the day – and there was an extra cost of something like 20 Francs to use it.

So, if you wanted to use the shower, you had to go down to reception, pay 20F so they would turn the hot water on and then go up and have your shower, which was a bit of a pain. But it was an interesting experience – and, at least, you could actually have a shower.

For a budget tourist hotel, it was in a very good position. It was in the 18th Arrondissement just on the edge of the main tourist area and within easy reach of all the sights.

From looking at a street map of Paris now, I can't quite identify where the hotel was but it was on a nice quiet, colourful, side street that led straight down to the main attractions. It was slightly downhill all the way and you basically just kept going in a straight line and you eventually ended up at the Seine.

The weather was nice and warm the whole time we were there - and not too hot – so it was great for walking and sightseeing.

From what I can hazily recall, over the course of our stay, we did the following:

- Walked along the River Seine and saw Notre Dame Cathedral and the famous book sellers along the river side.

- Climbed up a huge amount of steps (270 according to Wikipedia...) to visit the Sacré Coeur and had a general poke about the arty quarter of Montmartre

- Visited the Louvre Museum just as it was about to close for the evening and rushed through it to get to see the Mona Lisa. This world-famous hugely valuable painting was practically hidden behind protective glass, rather small and generally very disappointing.

- Visited the Arc De Triomphe and climbed to the top.

- Had a look around the Place Pigalle and saw the Moulin Rouge. We didn't go in as you had to book and it was horrendously expensive. I also got propositioned by a prostitute on a street corner.

Needless to say, we also went and saw the Eiffel Tower – which is a bit of a must when you go to Paris.

Now, for anybody who hasn't been, there are two (probably more – but two as far as I am concerned) ways of seeing the Eiffel Tower. The first one is to literally go to where it is positioned in the Champ de Mars on the south bank of the Seine opposite the Pont D'Iena, between the Quai Jacques Chirac and the Avenue Gustav Eiffel.

There, you can look up and marvel at the sheer size of this iconic construction, take the lift ride and stairs up to the top and enjoy the views across the city.

That is absolutely great and a wonderful experience if you are able to do it – but, because you are so close to it, you don't actually get a very good view of the Eiffel Tower from there.

To get the best overall view of the Eiffel Tower – ie the one you tend to see in all the photos - you need to take the Metro to Trocadero and view it from outside the Palais de Chaillot.

From there you have the Esplanade de Trocadero and the gardens and fountains laid out before you and the brilliant view of the Tower across the river.

So we did that as well.

November 1988 to March 1989: Sima Torcy

You might think that, having spent three weeks in St Etienne earlier in the year and then a week in Paris in the summer, I might have had enough of France by now. Not a bit of it - the biggest adventure was yet to come!

But let's go back a little bit first as my first involvement with Sima Torcy came a little earlier in the year.

Just to clarify - Sima Torcy is the name of a printing company. Torcy is also the name of the town in the area of Marne La Vallée, which is 20km to the east of Paris.

Marne La Vallée is probably better known to most people as the location of the EuroDisney / Disneyland Paris resort, although that only opened in 1992 and was still empty fields when I was in that area.

Anyway, Sima Torcy was an existing customer of Baker Perkins and they already had an old G16 press which had been running well for several years. They had ordered a new G14 press with C2 merged stream folder to be installed in the same building and this was ready to be shipped at the end of October 1988.

Before the press was shipped to the customer, some of Sima's engineers and printers came over to England for training courses.

Baker Perkins had a good customer training programme in those days run by Roger Davis. In theory, it was a chargeable course, but in practice it was usually an "add on" that was given away to customers as an extra sweetener when they were buying a new press.

Depending on who was attending the courses and what they needed to look at, there were classroom sessions, opportunities to look at the equipment being built in the fitting shops and visits to established press sites to see the machinery in operation. It was also possible to call in any members of the design staff or commissioning teams who were in the office to discuss specific queries or issues that might come up.

Because you couldn't always rely on the customer's personnel speaking English, it was often necessary to have an interpreter sit in on the training courses.

The difficulty there was that you couldn't have just anybody who happened to speak French because, if they didn't understand the specialised printing terminology and know a little about the products, you'd spend considerably more time explaining it to them than actually answering the engineers' questions.

Case Study: "Lost" In Translation...

Just as an example of this – and this is going off the point somewhat but it is still vaguely relevant - after I had left Rockwell in 1995 to become a hard up University student, I began offering translation services as a freelancer.

I had handled most of the French language work for Baker Perkins and Rockwell for the previous 8 years or so and was fully conversant with their products and all the terminology.

Now, language professionals will tell you that you should only ever translate or interpret into your own native language but the various companies here knew me and my background and were always happy to use the French texts that I had produced. I could, after all, always ask the French agent if I was really stuck with something but that hardly ever happened.

One Friday afternoon, when I was looking forward to a leisurely weekend, I was sent a fax by a hot air dryer manufacturing company – who I won't name as who it was doesn't really matter.

They were based in Germany but had a UK office where I knew several of the sales people, and they asked me if I could translate a quotation for them from English into French by Monday as they needed it urgently.

I said "fine" and did it over the weekend so they had it to meet their deadline on Monday.

On Monday lunchtime, I had another fax through saying that my translation was unsuitable and full of errors – and, as a result, they weren't going to pay my invoice – which was about £300.

It turned out that they had sent my translation through to their FRENCH OFFICE first thing for them to check it. Now, I didn't even know that they had a French office and, now knowing that they did, my initial question was why didn't they get them to do it in the first place and save me slaving over it all weekend?

The answer – although it remained unspoken - was clear enough. The French office had probably closed for the weekend and nobody else wanted to spend all weekend doing this damned translation, so they turned to me.

Anyway, they did, at least, send me back a copy of my translation with their French office's corrections scrawled all over it. But despite the huge amount of presumably red (although you can't tell colours from a fax) pen, there was hardly a thing wrong with it.

The problem arose from the term that I had used for the dryer which in French is "un sécheur" – a masculine noun.

We always called it "un sécheur" in everything that we did – it was so called on all quotations and leaflets - and, as far as I could tell, so did everybody else – including the French firm MEG, who also made dryers.

But for some reason, the person who had checked my translation had got it into their head that a dryer was "une sécheuse" – a feminine noun - and not "un sécheur" (masculine).

This had the unfortunate knock-on effect that, every time the dryer was mentioned in the text, any pronouns that conveyed the gender of the word - like "il" or "elle", "le" or "la" and "un" or "une" - were consequently incorrect.

The same went for all the verb agreements - "**la** séche**use** sera install**ée**" instead of my "le sécheur sera installé" and so on.

Bearing in mind that practically the whole text was about le sécheur instead of their notionary sécheuse, that made for a whole load of red ink - even though it was otherwise totally correct in itself!

I eventually complained to the guy that I knew in their UK sales office and asked him to intervene on the basis that:

a) they should have got their French office to do the translation in the first place,

b) whoever heard of a dryer being called a sécheuse, and

c) I had still done all the work over the weekend to meet their ridiculous deadline and there was nothing actually wrong with the translation anyway.

I offered to knock £50 off the invoice as a gesture of goodwill and my bill was eventually paid and, surprisingly enough, I never heard from that company again!

So that is why you can't have just any old body doing translating or interpreting for a highly specialised technical subject.

And I still maintain that a hot air drier on a printing press in French is masculine!

A Happy PS – The Dog Food Dryer!

There is, in fact, a happy post script to this traumatic dryer translation story. It is jumping ahead a bit but it makes sense to include it here while we are on that particular subject.

In around 2000, a company from Stamford near Peterborough contacted me out of the blue and asked if I would translate something into French for them.

It turned out that some of their staff had previously worked at Baker Perkins PMC before it had shut down and, as such, they knew about my background and capabilities.

This company were part of an American concern who also manufactured hot air dryers who were supplying one to a (well-known...) pet food manufacturer in France – and they needed the operator's manual translating into French.

Being well and truly self employed by this time, I immediately said yes - but with the caveat that I knew nothing at all about the manufacture of dog food.

They reassured me that the dryer was basically the same as one for a printing press - ie a long gas fired oven - and the only real difference being that the product to be dried was transported through it on a conveyor belt.

I then pointed out the problem that I'd had with the other dryer manufacturer and their French office a few years earlier - stating that it was generally accepted linguistic policy only to translate into one's own native language - but they were untroubled by any of this.

They knew me, they were adamant that they wanted ME to do it and they would be perfectly happy with whatever I produced – which was nice...

It was quite a big job, as they had never done a dryer for France before and was some 200 pages or so of technical manual, along with the instructional drawings that needed labelling, various charts, spare parts lists, electrical diagrams and so on.

The material came through to me in drabs and drabs - as it became available for this customer's machine - by email and occasionally courier package, from both the Stamford people and the main office in the US so I was able to do it a bit at a time and pace myself.

I sent each section back when it was ready, to make sure they were happy with it and to enable me to adjust anything they didn't think was right before it got copied over and over - but, with them being an American company who only ever dealt with everything in English, they were over the moon!

It took several weeks to complete and, over that time, I was able to put my full acquired knowledge about horizontal gas fired hot air dryers and their operation from over the years to good use - and I also learnt how to engage and adjust conveyor belts in French and what the various processing times for different types of dog food were.

And I have to say that I never had the slightest problem with this customer whatsoever - nor any negative feedback back from the French end-user.

It was a very good earner for me – around £1500 – and if I could have picked up a job like that a few times a year, that would have been perfect.

Sadly, the world and its technology began to change around that time and since then I have tended to have smaller translation jobs.

But it was a nice compliment that this company - and their French client - were perfectly happy with my French language operators manual for their animal feed dryer.

*****

Anyway, back to the Sima Torcy press installation in 1988 where I was also well and truly in charge of what got called what...

I wasn't involved in the interpreting for the day to day running of the training courses for Sima. That task fell to Maurice Lubbock who was an installation engineer and also spoke fluent French.

He was actually the son of a Lord (the 4th Baron Avebury, according to The Peerage.com) but, unfortunately for him, wasn't the first born son and therefore didn't inherit the title. Despite being of noble birth, Maurice never put on any airs and graces and was also very pleasant and helpful as far as I was concerned.

As I recall, two sets of Sima engineers came over for training courses - each for a week's duration.

It had been decided that I was going to go out to the press installation to help out with the languages and generally gain experience. I have no idea how this actually came about or whose idea it was. If there was a meeting about me / it, I was certainly not included in it and I never saw any memos on the subject.

Whether there was some grandiose master plan going on behind the scenes to expose me to all areas of the company, a strategic flowchart on somebody's office wall - I knew nothing of that - and nobody else ever said anything either. As with lots of things in this life, it just seemed to happen all on its own.

Anyway, because I was going to be going out there and having to deal with these engineers, Maurice brought them up to the office to introduce me to them.

There was always a lot of entertaining involved with these training courses – which we will deal with in more detail later – to avoid leaving a group of engineers bored in a hotel room for a week in a foreign country, and the up-shot of this was that I was invited out to dinner with Maurice and the French engineers.

Now, with Maurice being well brought up, you can imagine that we didn't just go out for a pizza... we went to the very swish, very expensive Bistro in town, where I had never been before.

As it was my first time out with customers on behalf of the company, I was very nervous – and it was also the first time that I had been to a restaurant of that calibre with quite so many knives and forks on the place settings!

Luckily, fine dining was very much Maurice's "milieu" and he put me – and the other guys - completely at ease over what to do with what without making a huge fuss about anything.

For example, when a huge serving of spare ribs arrived for everybody - and I peered at them in horror wondering how to go about eating them in a polite manner - he just casually announced without looking at anybody in particular "I don't know about you, but I tend to just pick these up and chew on them...."

And the atmosphere around the table immediately relaxed.

It was a really enjoyable evening with very little work chat. The food was sumptuous – if a little rich for my less-educated tastes back then - Maurice knew exactly what wines to have with what and was a charming host all together.

The following week, there was an evening when Maurice wasn't available to take the next group out so, having presumably given a good enough account of myself the previous week, I was sent out on my own to take them out.

We went to the Bistro again – as it was fairly close to the Bull Hotel in the town centre, where they were staying and therefore very easy to get to – and I took my office colleague Anne Castellano with me for support, as she also spoke very good French.

The route from Peterborough to Torcy (Source: www.google.com/maps)

The Adventure Begins

So, the day finally arrived when I was to travel to France to help at the Sima Torcy press installation.

I can't remember the exact dates but I think it was the end of October / beginning of November and I stayed there for most of the month.

I drove down to Paris with Grenville Cousins, who was an FED installation engineer and I already knew him from when he had worked in the PMC fitting shop. We had an early start as the ferry was booked for late morning and it took about 3 hours to drive from Peterborough to Dover.

Although I had been on ferries on coach trips when I was younger – and as a foot / rail passenger - this was the first time that I had ever gone through the process of driving onto a car ferry as an involved adult and it was really exciting to do.

Once we were on board the ferry, Grenville and I headed for the bar area and there we met up with two more installation engineers – Mark Stickland and Tony Santoro, who were also heading for Sima.

I knew Mark as well as he had also previously worked as a fitter in the Fitting Shop – but Tony was new to the company. He was a "Peterborough Italian" – the significance of which will become clear later on...

It was quite a nice pleasant day - sunny but cold, so not bad for travelling. The Channel crossing went OK and I managed to not feel seasick once. We returned to our respective cars and arranged to meet up at the hotel later in the day.

Driving in a car as an adult is greatly different to being on a coach as a child as you take more notice of your surroundings – so it was a really enjoyable and interesting drive from Calais down to Paris.

That journey took another 3 or 4 hours so it was lucky that Grenville was good company and we found lots of things to talk about. We arrived at the hotel at Croissy-Beaubourg in the early evening just as it was getting dark.

Now, if you look on the map at that particular area now, it has changed beyond all recognition from how it was when I was there. The arrival of Eurodisney has seen all sorts of new hotels, attractions and other infrastructure pop up around there whereas when we arrived at Croissy on that autumnal evening in 1988, it was still a quiet village surrounded by countryside.

In fact, the closest I have ever got to being at Eurodisney Marne La Vallée was to see a solitary sign on a fence in front of a huge empty field announcing that that was where it was going to be.

Strangely enough, there used to be a similar sign on a fence on the outskirts of Corby in Northamptonshire as they had previously planned to build Eurodisney on the site of the old steelworks there. That was before somebody had the bright idea that people might actually prefer to go to Paris than some small remote town in the middle of England full of Scottish people...

The hotel we stayed in – and I won't mention its name just in case it is still operating, and I hope they are – was a nice quiet country old fashioned place.

I had actually picked it out and made all the booking arrangements – telling them that a large group of us would be coming on and off for several months and that a special deal would help us decide where to stay etc. And it was a very nice place.

It would have been very nice for a relaxing overnight stay if you were on your way to the south of France – or in the area for a short business trip - but it was bit over twee and bijou for a group of engineers to unwind in after a hard day's work for a long period of time.

The rooms weren't overly spacious, for example, and the televisions in the rooms weren't overly big.

The bath in my room – I don't know about anybody else's – wasn't actually a full size bath at all. It was short and deep with a ledge that you had to sit on to get in properly. While you could at least have a bath in it, it wasn't really ideal.

Plus the food in the restaurant was all very "à la carte" and rich and sophisticated. It wasn't really a sort of "steak and chips and beer place" so I quickly realised that it wouldn't really be suitable for our purposes.

As soon as we could, we all decamped to the nearby Novotel at Collegien, which was more the sort of thing that they guys were used to.

The next morning we got up and drove into the printing plant for the first time. Grenville had been there before – either the installation on the old G16 press a few years earlier or on more recent service visits - so he had a reasonable idea of his way around.

We were given a nice quiet room along the corridor from the main offices where we could keep our things. It had cupboards and a central table and chairs where we could sit down and write faxes and reports as required - and also to chill out during break times.

It was a lot more comfortable than the old portakabin that we'd had at IGPM but that had been in a new building that wasn't finished whereas now we were in a fully functioning company.

Mark Leaning had arrived later the evening before so there were 5 BP engineers – Mark, Sticks, Tony, Gren and a contractor called Graham, plus me. I am fairly sure that Chris Rojek came along as well on the electrical side but I am not sure at what point he turned up.

The scene was set for the delivery of the press equipment.

Preparing The Building.

Before you can install a multi-million pound printing press in a building, a lot of preliminary work needs to be done - well in advance.

Months, if not years, beforehand, the building will have been measured by an architect - or some other specialist engineer - using precision instruments and a building drawing produced. Based on the building drawing, a decision would be made as to what size of press would fit into it and where it would stand in relation to the existing infrastructure.

Once the configuration of the press was agreed upon – along with its various auxiliary components (we'll come to those later...) the press manufacturer would then produce a layout drawing of the press and show how it would fit into the space in the building.

After the specification was agreed and the order placed, the customer could begin to prepare their building for receiving the press.

The floor is the most crucial part of these preparations as, if you are going to bolt and cement a huge heavy expensive piece of equipment down - and have it running at 50.000 revolutions per hour, day and night for many years, you have to be sure that the base is secure.

In most cases, (this was so in the 80s and 90s when I was there, anyway) a new reinforced concrete floor is laid in the customer's building and the press manufacturer provides a detailed drawing showing what weights and stresses it will have to be able to cope with.

Once the concrete floor is in place, it has to have holes drilled in where the press components will be installed. Here again, the press manufacturer provides the customer with a detailed drawing showing exactly what holes - circumference, depth etc need to be drilled where in order for the press to drop into place.

As well as all this, the customer also needs to provide piped services to particular points on the press layout. A separate "services" drawing shows exactly where water, oil, drainage, compressed air, electricity and gas need to be piped to so that the installation engineers can merely hook up when required. This is something else that all needs doing well in advance of the arrival of the actual press equipment.

Delivering & Unloading

I don't remember the exact sequence of events here as it was all a very long time ago and quite a novel experience so, if I get this out of order a bit, I do apologise. This isn't meant to be a highly detailed account, it's just my recollections and observations so, even if it is not 100% accurate, it will still give you a general idea.

Basically there will have been a delivery schedule so that only one large piece of equipment was delivered at a time. We had heavy lifting subcontractors who used cranes and forklifts to lift the machines off the delivery lorry and to position them as close as possible to where they needed to go in the press line.

Now is about as good a time as any to explain about the different major components of one of our printing presses. They might not necessarily have been delivered and installed in this order, but there is a logical progression here along the length of the press.

Reelstand

The first item that we used to sell as part of the press was the reelstand. This basically holds a large roll of paper (up to 1.5m or so in diameter) that is then fed through the press to have the images printed onto it.

The reelstand was one of the "auxiliary" components that Baker Perkins sold as part of the press package but that we actually ordered from another specialist company.

At Sima, the reelstand was supplied by a Dutch company called Stork-Contiweb, but we also sometimes supplied reelstands from Butler – a Swiss company - and MEG from France, depending on the customer's choice.

A reelstand is often called a "splicer" or a "flying paster" and the clever bit is where you can change from a roll of paper that is about to run out to new one without having to stop the machine and go through the start up process all over again.

The new roll is rotated until it is running at the same speed as the press is operating at and then a clever device attaches the new web of paper to the old, cuts off the stream coming from the old roll and the press keeps on running, thus saving a lot of time and materials. This is known as a splice.

Check it out on YouTube under "flying paster" – there are numerous examples of this fascinating operation.

Infeed.

The constant tension infeed is supplied by the same manufacturer as the reelstand. Its description says it all, really. This device is to make sure that the stream of paper (the "web", as it is known in printing terms like "web offset") is kept at a constant tension as it is run through the printing units. This is very important for the quality of the printed image.

Print Units.

The print units are the part of the press that do the actual printing. They have the printing plates mounted on cylinders that rotate and this prints the image on the web of paper as it passes through. Each revolution of the plate produces a new image on the paper, and on a G14 press, each of these images represents a 16-page section.

There is a lot more to it than that, obviously, but that's all you need to know for now. We can look at the printing units in more detail later on when we get to the commissioning stage at Sima in March 1989.

The Baker Perkins presses tended to have 4 print units and each unit printed a different colour.

The first was black, the second cyan, then magenta and the last in the line was yellow. I might have got cyan (blue) and magenta (red) in the wrong order there - but the other two are definitely right. With a clever mixing of inks you can produce all the colours required from those 4 basic primes. Yellow ink is used the most in full colour printing so that is applied last.

Some presses actually have 5 units because the customer might want to add specialised extra colours like gold or silver and some presses have 8 units - ie two sets of 4, either in-line or duplex - running twice as many paper webs for more flexibility or greater production capabilities.

The majority of the print units that were sold when I was involved were G14 and G16 units. I seem to think that the model numbers originally came from the printing speed on the units ie: a paper speed of 1400 and 1600 feet per minute.

However, as we began having more to do with Europe over time, the web speeds became expressed in meters per second with an average of something like 8 or 9 m/sec - and overall production was assessed in terms of 1000 copies per hour, of which around 50.000 was the norm in the mid to late 1980s.

A G14 was a 16 page unit – which means that every revolution of the plate cylinder produced a flat image on the paper containing 16 pages – 8 pages on the upper side (recto) and 8 pages on the lower side (verso).

A G16 – like they already had at Sima - was a double circumference machine that could produce 32 pages from one revolution. In simplified terms, you would attach 2 x G14 size printing plates around the G16 plate cylinder and could then produce 1 x 32 page copy - or twice as many 16 page copies - to give a higher production rate.

Other print unit models that were produced using my time were:

The G16CW: CW was short for "commercial width". This was basically same as a G16 unit but was 50% wider to produce 48-page copies.

The G12: This was a new 16 page unit that was introduced at the Drupa exhibition in Düsselfdorf in 1986. An experimental G12 press (1200 fpm) with C1 folder was sold to Heron Print in Essex but its new, innovative - and much publicised - "fibre optic control system" had a lot of teething troubles and it affected customer confidence in the market place.

According to Ian Douglas's excellent personal memoir on the Baker Perkins Historical Society website (bphs.net), only 7 G12 presses were ever sold, including three into N. America and one to replace the original Heron units.

The G25: This was the next generation of presses that was brought in during the 1990s with a much higher printing speed. These were designed to operate at 10 m/sec or 75.000 copies an hour (presumably 2500 feet per min) to keep up with similar machines that had been developed by the competition.

The problem for us was that the G25 had been designed for and introduced into the North American market first, where the paper print sizes were different and, therefore, the size of the print units wasn't suitable for sale to customers in the UK and Europe.

Let me try and explain this without making it too complicated.

In North America they still use imperial measurements instead of metric which, in normal everyday circumstances, I would say "good on them" but, in terms of printing and publishing, it's a complete pain in the arse.

If you have ever seen or bought an American produced book or magazine, you'll have noticed that it is a different size and shape to those produced in the UK or Europe.

We now have standardised paper sizes measured in mm and based on A3, A4 and so on -whereas they measure their paper sizes in inches and are based around the old Quarto format.

With regards to the paper products that Baker Perkins customers in Europe wanted to be able to print, the majority of the work was A4 sized colour magazines or advertising inserts. This was known as Quarter Page because of how it was produced in the folding mechanism.

The next product size up was Tabloid - which is the size that most newspapers are nowadays - and the format was equivalent to A3 size. This was produced in the same way as above but without the addition of the quarter fold.

Another popular size was what the Americans called "Digest Size" – which was, literally, the A5 size of Readers Digest - and that was produced by doing a "double parallel" fold.

So the G14 units that were being installed at Sima Torcy would be capable of printing one 16 page A4 copy per revolution or one 8 page tabloid product, depending on how the image was laid out on the printing plate and how the folder was set up.

Now, in order to be able to print these differing product formats, the press equipment supplied to the US had to be a different size to the UK / Europe version.

The standard cut off size (ie: circumference of the plate cylinder), which determined the vertical height of the finished copy, was 580mm and the width of the print unit and the paper that it was to handle was 914mm.

For UK and European presses, the standard cut off size was 630mm and the width 965mm.

Now, 5 cm either way may not sound like much in laymen's terms but in terms of precision engineering it made a huge difference.

It meant that all of the individual parts of the press that were dependent on the overall width of the machine or on the circumference of the cylinders had to be designed, engineered and manufactured as completely separate items for each size of press.

In manufacturing terms, this meant that individual components of the printing press were produced as either "cut off related " or "non cut off related" parts and were produced in the machining shops in batches according to requirement forecasts.

Aside from the basic sizes of various pieces of metal, there were / are a lot of other differences between a press that was built for the American market and one for the European market.

American customers tended to favour a "brush dampening system" which used brush rollers to apply the dampening solution to the printing plate whereas UK / European presses had "continuous dampening" which used a different type of roller arrangement.

The electrical voltages and current types are completely different in America so all of the electrical components and wiring had to be designed and installed to suit that environment.

Plus the safety requirements were greatly different between continents so failsafe mechanisms, safety guards, control panel layouts, warning signs and stop buttons all had to be especially designed and manufactured according to the country they were going to.

All of this involved a huge amount of man hours and costs and, unfortunately, the American Rockwell International parent company that owned Baker Perkins at that time was not prepared to invest those costs into re-engineering the American version G25 press for the European market.

The G25 print units were being manufactured in the US and were only available in US sizes. With the commercial printing industry being so cutthroat, there was no way that a European customer would accept an extra long delivery time to wait for the 630mm cut off press to be designed for the G25.

In what was a very frustrating vicious circle, Rockwell wouldn't release the resources without customer orders coming in to help pay for it, so the G25 never made it into Europe – and we were left without a competitive new machine to sell.

The G44: This was a "cross grain" press unit that was also developed in the late 1980s/ early 1990s.

If my recall and understanding is correct – and it may very well not be as I had very little involvement with this press - the idea of cross grain was that the image was printed the other way round on the paper so that width determined the length of the copy instead of the cut off. The advantage of this, I believe, was to offer more flexibility of format.

The first G44 press was installed at Kingfisher Web in Peterborough in 1991 and, according to Ian Douglas, two further G44 presses were sold to North America before the product line was discontinued.

So now you know all that you need to - for the time being - about print units – of which 4 were unloaded and positioned at Sima Torcy as part of their new G14 press installation.

Hot Air Dryer

The next large bit of kit in the press machinery line is the dryer – which we all now know is called "LE SECHEUR" in French!

This is basically a long horizontal gas-fired oven which the printed web of paper passes through in order for the ink to dry. This is what makes this particular process known as "heatset" printing. Other types of press use different inks - and no dryer - and that is called "coldset".

The length of the dryer depends on the web speed of the paper that needs to pass through it. So, for a slower press you'd have a shorter dryer - say 6 to 7 meters - and for a faster press, it would be 8 or 10 meters in length.

With pollution control becoming a big worldwide concern in the late 1980s and early 1990s, an optional device was added to a lot of dryers called an afterburner. Rather like a catalytic converter on car exhaust system this used a process to eliminate a certain amount of the toxic exhaust gasses that came out of the dryer and helped reduce emissions into the atmosphere.

I would imagine that, with all the progress that had been made in this area over the intervening decades, much of the hitherto add on "optional" afterburner technology will now be included in modern day hot air dryers as standard.

The dryer was another "auxiliary" item that we purchased from an outside supplier – normally TEC Systems, Vits or MEG. We tended to install the equipment on site and they sent out their own engineers out later to commission and test it before it went into production.

Chill Rolls.

The printed paper web is very hot when it emerges from the dryer so it needs to be cooled down before it goes into the folder. This is where the chill rolls come in.

Chill rolls were huge 20" diameter heavy stainless steel rollers that had chilled water piped through them. The paper web was wound around these rollers on its way between the dryer and the folder and it was through the contact with the chill rolls that it was cooled to a manageable temperature.

The chill rolls were manufactured by Baker Perkins and came in two sizes - 20" and (I think....) 16". Depending on the size and speed of the press, you would have either 4 or 6 rolls per web pass.

The Folder

The folder is the last main piece of the puzzle and, obviously, very important if you want to produce a finished magazine out of your flat piece of printed paper.

I have to hold my hand up here and say that I don't know as much about folders as I do about some of the other pieces of equipment. This is despite them having been built from scratch not 10 yards away from the office where I worked for 2 ½ years in the fitting shop, numerous customer visits – one of which I do certainly remember clambering all over a half finished folder on – plus two press start-ups. I can only assume that I have a mental block as far as far folders are concerned. So there you are. Sack me!

The principal workhorse folder that was the mainstay of the Baker Perkins presses in the 1980s and early 1900s when I was there was the C2 folder, which worked with G14 and G16 presses.

C2 stands for "double chopper" folder and this had two chopper mechanisms that performed the final fold on a quarter page copy before it was delivered onto the folder's exit conveyors, of which it also had 2.

The C2 folder was a huge piece of equipment - about 4 meters high - and was very heavy. The printed paper was fed into it via an infeed, which had different variants depending on the customer's requirements.

One was a "ribbon infeed", which had wheels with sharp blades that slit the incoming paper lengthways into strips and then laid them one on top of the other ready to go into the folding mechanism.

The other was a "former infeed" which was a large highly polished triangle shape with a very sharp point at the end.

By passing along this, the paper web was folded in half as it was drawn into the main body of the folder.

The "former nose" at the point of the former infeed was razor sharp and very dangerous. I know this for a fact as installation engineer Albert Marriott cut his hand on it at Sima and I had to go with him to hospital to have it looked at.

As far as I can remember - mental blocks permitting – a rotating cylinder with a knife blade across its width cut the incoming web to the right length as it came down in to the main body of the folder from the infeed, and then a series of grip and tuck cylinders took hold of the copy and made the tabloid fold.

The copy then went through the chopper mechanism to make the quarter fold and the quarter page signatures were carried out on the delivery conveyors.

The other types of folder that were used on Baker Perkins presses at this time were:

C1 Folder

This was a "single chopper" folder that had been designed to work with the G12 press although, as a 16 page folder, it was also used on G14 presses. It was a lot smaller than a C2 folder and had quicker product change over times abut otherwise did pretty much the same thing.   The G14 press at IGPM had a C1 folder.

F2 Folder

This was a smaller folder with a double former infeed (hence the designation F2) which was only capable of producing quarter page copies. It was cheaper to produce than the C2 and was popular with early American sales of the G14 presses.

C2 Merged Stream Folder

This was the same as a regular double chopper C2 folder but it had a single delivery conveyor, ie the two output streams merged. The benefit for the customer was that they only needed one set of conveying equipment to transport the finished copies away to the finishing line. The G14 press at Sima Torcy had a C2 Merged Stream folder.

HS (High Speed) Folder

This was the next generation folder that was designed to work with G14, G16 and G25 presses and run at a much higher speed (up to 2500 fpm) than the C2 folder.

It had a lot of technical advances and included automated product change over which only took about five minutes as opposed to ages doing it manually on an old C2.

Good though it was, the HS folder was a huge piece of kit and its selling price came in at about 1 million pounds in the early 1990s – that's without looking at the rest of the press equipment.

Because of all the difficulties involved in selling Baker Perkins presses in the mid-1990s, only 4 HS folders were sold.

So basically, the press equipment that we were installing at Sima Torcy consisted of

- Stork reelstand and infeed
- 4 x Baker Perkins G14 print units
- Tec Systems dryer
- Chill Rolls
- C2 MS Folder
- Harland Simon main drive
- Plus all the electrical cabinets, control desks and miles of cabling needed to make all of that work.

- Plus all the platforming, steps, ladders, handrails, safety guards and main drive shaft sections that connect all the various press elements together.

There are a lot of other important pieces of equipment that make up a printing press that I haven't gone into here.

Things like

- Web break detectors that automatically shut down the press if the paper breaks.
- Web severers that cut the paper in case of a break so that it doesn't jam up the machine and cause serious damage
- Colour register control system that keeps the image in focus between units
- Automatic oil lubrication system
- Ink supply system
- Dampening recirculation system
- Air turns to guide the printed web from the chill rolls into the folder infeed
- Silicone applicator for high quality glossy magazines
- Inline gluing system
- Plate punch and bender so that the printing plate fits properly onto the plate cylinder
- Plate scanner to preset the inking settings
- Plus all the conveyors and finishing line equipment, which is the customer's responsibility.

I could go on - but you get the idea....

So over the coming weeks, all this equipment was put into its correct place, lined and levelled using highly specialised telescopic apparatus, then bolted and cemented to the floor.

Then everything was all connected together, all the other periphery equipment installed and by late February March, we were finally ready to start the machine up.

PB with Tony Santoro at the press installation at Sima Torcy. From this photo you can see the height of the printing units – and also the reelstand in the background.

What I Did....

So what did I actually do while all this was going on?

Well, there was a large amount of hanging around waiting for something to happen. I did a lot of holding spanners or fetching work lamps and a lot of communicating with French people, which is what I was actually there for.

Overall, I was at Sima for about a month in October / November at the start of the installation and then another 6 weeks in February / March ready for the commissioning. To be perfectly honest, a lot of it has merged into one in my memory so, rather than trying to be too specific about what happened when – as it doesn't really matter after all this time (it's not as if I am writing a report...) - I'll just give you some general reminiscences.

Tool Shop Visit.

The first thing that really sticks in my mind was one morning in our first week when I went out with Grenville to buy some tools and other bits and pieces that he needed for a job he was trying to get done.

We found a tool shop on a nearby industrial estate and when we got to the counter, he asked me to ask the chap for a "10 mil tap".

Now, I am not mechanically trained but I did, at least, know what a tap was from the time that I had spent in the office in the fitting shop. However, 10 years of learning lots of different things in French from the age of 11 had not prepared me to know what a tap was actually called in the language.

So I smiled awkwardly at the helpful counter assist and launched into a long spiel in French trying to explain the function of this tool that I wanted – with appropriate French looking gestures added in for good measure - something along the lines of "it's a round tool for cutting a internal thread on the inside of a hole in a piece of metal..."

The Franc eventually dropped and the guy said "Ah – un taraud!" with great excitement, as if we were on a TV quiz show.

I quickly said – a what? - "C'est quoi...?" – desperate to learn this new word that I had worked so hard to find out – and he repeated "Un Taraud".

"Et ça s'écrit comment?" I asked him to write it down so as to further cement the term in my noggin and he duly did so: T A R A U D.

So we tortuously worked down the rest of Gren's list - a few of the things I knew already and a few I didn't, but we generally managed to make ourselves understood – and, after a shopping trip that probably took 4 times as long as it would have done at home, we returned back to the site to get on with the job.

Now, if you have never found yourself in a totally foreign environment where you have to closely hang on every single word to know what is going on - and have to think and speak in a foreign language for sustained periods - you would never believe how tiring it can be.

This is why professional interpreters at conferences and places like the United Nations only work for a set period and then take a break – and I can fully understand how they can burn out by the time they are 30!

So I was zonked by this experience and went to have a cup of tea up in our quiet room and make a phone call to the office. Don't forget that, while I was there doing all the site interpreting, I was also supposed to be keeping an eye on my Peterborough office work as well, so it all took a bit of organising.

I got through to Steve Kimber in the Field Engineering office on the phone – I don't remember what the reason for the call was – but he asked me how things were going. I casually mentioned in passing that I'd had a busy and tiring morning going round suppliers trying to purchase tools, thinking that, as he was learning French and German himself with the company, he might be sympathetic.

Instead, he put his hand over the phone - but I could still hear him quite clearly in the background - and he shouted out across the office:

"Hey – Paul's been out on a jolly all morning with Grenville...!"

I appreciate that it was only "Field Engineer's humour", which, on the Richter Scale of piss-taking, probably falls somewhere between gallows humour and playground pranks - but if he hadn't been 370km away, I would have happily throttled him!

But due the various hoops that I had to jump through on that first morning to make myself understood, I have NEVER forgotten that the French word for a tap is "Un Taraud"!

Afternoon tea with Micheline Left to Right: Chris Rojek, PB, Harry Leggatt, Micheline Guyon, Graham Jeffrey, Tony Santoro, Mark Stickland

Afternoon Tea With Micheline

The people who I had the most to do with at Sima were:

Jean Coty - who was the chief engineer, in charge of all plant maintenance and overseeing the installation for the new press from the customer's point of view.

Thierry Lobjoie - who was the maintenance engineer and who I had previously met when he had come over to Peterborough for one of the training courses.

Sandrine – who was the receptionist and in charge of the phones so she always helped when we needed to make a call or send a fax. She was also very helpful on local geography as to what was where.

Franck Rumilly – who was the No1 Printer who was learning to operate the new G14 press. There were 3 printers all together and I spent quite a lot of time with them as we were setting up the press and starting test runs.

Claude Pelletanche – who was the overall boss of the printing plant. He was always very smart with a double breasted suit, slicked back hair and moustache and he looked like somebody out of a 1940s French film. He was always very polite, respectfully aloof, and used to slightly nod his head and snap "Pelletanche" as he introduced himself to you.

& Micheline Guyon.

Now I can't for the life of me tell you what Micheline actually did at Sima. She was *possibly* Pelletanche's PA and she certainly spent most of the time swanning around looking chic, managerial and important. Now, I mean that in a very positive way, by the way, as I got on very well with her and she was always very helpful to me.

And she had her own office, whereas the chief accountant, par contre – a lady whose name I have since forgotten but I did have few chats with - was out in the main open plan office along with everybody else.

I spent a lot of time chatting with Micheline while I was at Sima - and when I left, she very kindly gave me a Dictionary of French slang words which she wrote in the front of and which I still have.

I had coffee with Micheline a few times in her office (yes - just coffee, obviously ...) and we used to chat about all sorts of things.

One thing that the French were fascinated about was the English and their afternoon tea. They had all noticed that mid-afternoon we would all stop whatever we were doing for 10 or 15 minutes and all congregate around our work bench and brew up a cuppa.

Now, back in the time I am talking about – and I don't know what it's like there now – but back then, the French didn't understand tea and didn't know how to make it properly. Their idea of "tea" was Lipton Yellow Label – which they thought was English, but you never actually saw it in England anywhere.

This Lipton's stuff was probably ok with a dash of lemon but having it with milk and sugar was a definite no no.

In fact, they didn't even have kettles in France when I went there in the 1980s. If you wanted to boil water to make a drink you did it in a saucepan. They may well have them now, but such is my own experience of France that, even now, I couldn't possibly tell you the French word for "kettle".

So, at one of these cosy coffee chats, Micheline was joking about the English and their "pause thé" and I suggested that she should come down and join us one afternoon. After all, we had proper PG Tips tea bags that somebody had brought over with them, a proper kettle and proper mugs – so what more could you ask for?

So she did – and a great time was had by all. I doubt she liked the tea - but that wasn't really the point of the exercise.

Coty Evening & Frogs Legs

One evening – quite early on in the installation – M Coty invited us out for a meal at a restaurant. This was very nice of him as he didn't have to but – as always - it meant a lot of extra work for me!

We didn't all go – there was just 4 of us and I think it was me, Grenville, Harry Leggatt and Mr Coty and he took us to a very nice, typically French, restaurant that he knew.

Aside from it being a very pleasant meal – and a nice opportunity to chat about non-work related topics in relaxed circumstances – there are two things that stick in my mind from this evening.

The first was when I lost the thread of a translation and ended up having two separate conservations at the same time.

Without wishing to appear unpleasant here, M Coty had a slightly odd way of speaking and seemed to mumble a lot of his words.

Although I was used to speaking to him, both on the telephone in the past and in his office and around the plant on the installation, I still had trouble understanding what he was saying from time to time – even face to face in a quiet office.

So you can just imagine what it was like trying to follow the conversation in a noisy restaurant with the wine freely flowing!

At some point during the evening, Mr Coty said something which I didn't quite hear properly or fully understand. I explained to the other guys what I thought he had said and they replied accordingly.

The next thing that Coty said clearly demonstrated that he was actually talking about something completely different to what I had told the guys - and this left me in a bit of a quandary....

Do I own up and admit that I had got something wrong – and thus shatter everybody's confidence in what a brilliant interpreter I was – or do I improvise and keep going with two different conversations in the hope that nobody notices?

So, drawing on Shakespeare's Henry IV Part 1 for inspiration - and deciding that discretion is the better part of valour, I spent a very uncomfortable few minutes carrying on two separate conversations at the same time, my mind working overtime trying to keep track of what I had said to who and what each side of the table thought we were talking about.

Luckily this didn't go on too long and the next course was brought to the table - or a new bottle of wine or something - and I was able to bring the split conversations abruptly to a close with some over the top exclamation like "Oh – doesn't that look nice...!" And I managed to get away with it.

The other memorable thing that happened on this particular evening was that I ate frog's legs for the one and only time in my life.

Now, French people are commonly known as "Frogs" because they eat frogs legs - and they also enjoy several other culinary peculiarities that we English people don't fully appreciate – such as snails, cow's brains and horse meat.

I have never knowingly eaten cow's brains or horse meat but I have had snails on a couple of occasions and quite enjoyed them – especially the ones that I had in the restaurant at the hotel in Croissy.

These were served in a very rich garlic and butter sauce, which I suppose was to mask the fact that they might otherwise taste like actual snails – a bit like curry sauce being originally invented to hide the fact that the meat was off – but I thought it was nice to have them for a change and to experience some proper French cuisine.

My one disappointment on the Croissy occasion was that, instead of being served in their shells like they traditionally are – you get given a sort of hat-pin type implement to wedge them out and eat them – these snails were nicely and very decoratively laid out on a round wooden board like a bread board with indentations in it. If anything, it looked a bit like one of those Solitaire board games with marbles that you often see in expensive gift shops.

I suppose the idea of serving it like that was so that you could just eat the snails with a fork and didn't get garlicky oily butter dripping all over your hands as you held the shell with one and tried to skewer the contents with the other, but it was a bit of a shame.

Anyway, back to the Frogs Legs. Contrary to popular beliefs, French people don't, in fact, eat Frog's Legs all the time. It is quite a rare delicacy these days and rather expensive to have. It is not a dish that can be found on every restaurant menu – snails are more common, or at least they were when I used to go to France – and I have hardly ever seen them offered in any of the places I have been to.

And this was why I was so keen to try them on the Coty evening as it might have been – and, in fact, turned out to be - the only opportunity I would ever have.

Now, for the benefit of anybody who has never eaten Frog's Legs before – and I realise that might realistically include most people… – this is what they were like:

The Frog's Legs (or "Cuisses de Grenouille" – frog's thighs - as they call them over there…) arrived in a bowl in some ragout of some sort.

They were very tiny and, unlike the Viking concept of grabbing a huge chicken leg in your fist and munching on it, you picked these up daintily between your thumb and forefinger and sucked the tiny amount of meat off the bone.

This was only ever going to be a mini appetiser dish as there was so little meat there and it looked rather much like match sticks with something odd on the end.

This is going to sound a bit clichéed - and I know that everybody always says when they try something different for the first time that it tastes like chicken – but this actually did taste like chicken!

Or as far as tiny little bits of chicken might taste if served in that self same strongly aromatic sauce, anyway.

But, having said that, when Lucy and I were living in Brussels in 2002, there was a local supermarket that sold exotic meats of the world. One day, just for a change, we decided to have a stew of Crocodile and Kangaroo meat – and that tasted just like chicken as well. So there you go!

Of course, I have to admit that I am slightly at a disadvantage here as I have no idea what natural Crocodile or Kangaroo meat is supposed to taste like, so I couldn't really say how authentic the Brussels stew was – any more then I could say how much like Frog's Legs my Frog's Legs actually tasted on the Coty evening - and that's probably a road better left untraveled, to be honest.

Now the best thing about eating snails - in a restaurant that is, not down the bottom of the garden – is that, by the time they have been cleaned, cooked and served up back in their shells or on a Solitaire board, they don't actually look like snails any more – just screwed up bits of meat.

If you actually had to eat a whole snail - with a tail and tentacles – that looked like Brian out of the Magic Roundabout, I doubt you'd really want to do it.

Ditto, the Viking chicken leg that we mentioned earlier. If you had to remove the leg from the chicken yourself - and if it still had feathers and feet and arteries attached to it, ie if it actually LOOKED like something that had just been ripped off a dead bird – would you really want to eat it? Of course you wouldn't.

A similar thing happened to me when I ordered a dish of octopus once in a restaurant by the seaside in Norfolk. I was expecting it to arrive looking like those rings of squid that you can get in most places, whereas the actual result looked much too much like intact little octopuses for me to be able to eat it.

And this brings me back to the gripping climax of my Frog's Legs story.

As I said, they didn't actually taste like Frog's Legs and they didn't really look like Frog's Legs so I was happily eating my French delicacy when I suddenly pulled something out of my bowl that hadn't been quite so meticulously prepared.

Instead of the little match sticks with a bit of meat at the top (this is why in French they are called "cuisses" - as it is only the thigh part that has any meat on it...), I got two matchsticks stuck together at the top. Not only were they attached together at the top to look like a pair, but they both had little feet at the bottom. In short – they looked like the back end of a tiny frog!

I almost freaked at this sudden vision and my first reaction was to scream in horror and throw the offending item away from me – far away - anywhere at all.

But realising where I was and who I was with, I bit my tongue, took a huge gulp of wine and carefully re-submerged the pair of legs and feet back into my ragout, in the hope of unseeing the image.

Obviously, the fact that I have been able to describe this to you in quite so much detail now shows that I never did unsee that particular image and the memory of suddenly discovering a bit of dead actual frog in my Frog's Legs has remained vivid ever since.

So as not to embarrass myself or insult the hospitality of our host, I tentatively dabbed my bread in the ragout and nibbled on that until the waiter came to clear the plates away – and we were eventually able to move onto the next course.

From left: Graham Jeffrey watching Mark Leaning and Tony Santoro marking out the floor for the Stork reelstand at Sima. In the background you can see the hook of the big crane used to lift the large components off the lorry trailers.

Above left: Sandrine – Sima Receptionist
Above right: Jean Coty, Micheline Guyon, Unknown.

Tea Break Time - Left to Right: Graham Jeffrey hard at work, Tony Santoro, Grenville Cousins, PB, Harry Leggatt & Mark Stickland.

Mark Leaning at the Sima press installation.

One of the funniest things I have ever heard – but you'd really have to have been there to see the joke – was when he saw Sticks pushing hard against a huge box at an inclined angle to budge it across the floor.

He pointed to him and shouted "Hey – there's Mark, leaning!"

Interpreting For Meetings

It's funny how over time you tend to forget a lot of the day to day things that happen and you only remember the dramatic or the traumatic.

My main memories of being at Sima Torcy all seem to be of me standing in front of somebody's desk in an office – rather like a naughty school boy – and being ranted at or complained to about something or other.

Nothing that I had actually done, mind you, or had any control over. It was just that I was the only person there who understood what anyone was saying and I had to spend most of my time conveying messages, checking on things and then going back with the relevant replies.

It can't all have been like that, obviously, otherwise I'd have been a complete nervous wreck by the end of the first week – but it certainly was an experience!

I do remember a particular meeting one afternoon, however, when EVERYBODY was there. Having just said "everybody" in capital letters, I don't really remember who was actually there, but it certainly seemed that anybody who was anybody was there.

Micheline was there, Pelletanche was there, Coty was there...

That was quite unusual as most discussions tended to take place relatively informally, often as a "brush-by" - like Ed Milliband once had with Barack Obama at the White House.

But this one saw everybody seated around a big table with pens and notepads and, as usual, I was very much in the middle of everything.

I seem to think that we were talking about the programme for the testing and start up of the press because I distinctly remember a really awkward moment when I was in the middle of explaining our printer Graham Perkins' philosophy on timescales – something along the lines of:

"If I am going to the pub, I don't tell my wife that I will be home at 10 and then come back at 11. I tell her that I'll be home at 12 and when I come back at 11 she'll be really happy that was I home early..."

And I realised – too late to backtrack - that what I was saying didn't come across any more professional and helpful in French than it sounded in English...

At another point, this meeting was completely derailed for a time when somebody took exception to my use of the word "si" – usually meaning "if" in French.

They took umbrage at the fact that I had appeared to "not believe" something that they were saying - and that I was in some way suggesting that it might not be true. This is taking nuance to the very extreme, by the way.

I can't even remember what we were talking about - but the completely bland and innocent phrase in question that I used was something like:

"Well if that's the case, we'll certainly get that fixed."

Which sounds pretty positive and reassuring to me but, for some reason, it seemed to have come across more as:

"Hmm, IF that's the case.... (ie a BIG if) we'll fix it..." which was certainly not what I intended at all.

Lucy has since - very helpfully - suggested that I could have said "en ce cas là" instead of "si" which would have removed any unintended element of doubt that I might have inferred. On the off chance that I ever find myself in a similar situation again, I shall try to remember this!

Oh - and at this same meeting I first came across the French slang word for work which is "boulot".

Chinese Restaurant

By the time I got back to Sima in January, the guys had found a few more places to go and eat out. One was a Chinese restaurant in Pontault Combault which was another quiet little village in the land of Brie.

I didn't like Chinese food. Or, at least, I didn't think I did. If it's something you're not used to, you tend to have that default reaction.

The only experience I had ever had of Chinese food in the past had been those Vesta meals that come in a packet and you re-hydrate the dried ingredients in a saucepan of water and curl up the crispy noodles in a hot frying pan, So - not really very authentic!

I used to imagine that I didn't like Indian food either, until Spiros Doukas took me to the Mumtaz in Peterborough town centre once on an evening out and I was very pleasantly surprised. And a similar thing happened with the Chinese food.

The guys said they were going to this restaurant they had found and, obviously, I was included in the invitation. As I didn't want to stop and eat at the hotel on my own, I figured that I had to go along.

Once we were seated, Chris Rojek explained to me that they ordered a whole load of different dishes – say 7 or 8 dishes if there were 5 people there, or whatever – plus lots of different starters and sides and everybody just passed them round and dug in.

The idea was, rather than just stick with the one dish you ordered yourself, you could try other things and it made the meal more fun and more sociable.

It was great for me as I didn't know what I liked and what I didn't, so I was able to try a little bit of everything and have been a big fan of Chinese food ever since.

Another advantage for us as a group was that, in France, Chinese restaurants tended to be a lot cheaper than they are in England so it was a good way to have a nice evening out and not break the bank.

Paris Evening Out

One evening during the week when we didn't have to stay late at the printing plant, several of us decided to drive into central Paris for the evening for a touristy look round.

Now this was the end of January - so it was dark and cold. During the whole of my time at Sima, it was always cold and this was a bit of a shock for me as I had never been in France in winter before.

I can't remember who went now – but there was only one car so there could only have been 5 of us at the most. I know Chris Rojek went – probably Phil Lycett, Me – and maybe Tony Santoro and Mark Stickland.

We headed for the Eiffel Tower and managed to get parked close by as it was midweek evening in January and there was nobody else about. The Tower was easy to find as it was brightly illuminated and it also had 1989 in huge lights to celebrate the 100th anniversary of its construction.

To our surprise, the Tower was still open so we all paid our fee and went up in the lift to the viewing platform. It was very windy at the top and you could feel the huge construction rocking slightly. The extra high bit at the top wasn't open – probably because of the wind – but we were at least able to look out across the fascinating Parisian panorama of..... FOG and DARKNESS!

Yes, that's right. Despite being up x hundred feet up in the air and overlooking one of the most beautiful cities in the world, we couldn't see a damn thing through the misty gloom – other than a few nearby streetlights. But at least we could say that we had been up the Eiffel Tower.

I have SEEN the Tower on many occasions on different visits but that is the only time that I have been up it so, even though we couldn't actually see anything, it remains a very special memory for me.

After all, I lived in Blackpool for 11 years and never once went to the top of the Blackpool Tower.

So, after our "unique" tower experience we ended up at the Place Pigalle. Don't ask me how we got there as I don't actually remember. I remember looking out from the viewing platform on the Tower and I remember walking along the cold empty streets around Pigalle but what happened in between is a bit of a mystery to me – and that's nothing to do with booze or drugs.

My geography of Paris isn't very good – I certainly didn't know where anything was driving-wise, as I had only ever got round by Metro on my previous visits.

Anyway, we were walking along a street that in the summer would be full of people but on this cold dark midweek night it was empty. We bought kebabs from a street seller, which were very nice if a little over indulged on the chilli sauce, and then found somewhere to sit and have a drink.

I can't remember the name of the place but it had some grandiose title like "Beers Of The World" or "House of Beers" and it claimed to have some ridiculous number - like 143 – of different beers on sale from all over the world.

The place was certainly decorated with beer-mats from all over the world and different brewery posters and it was quite eye catching as a theme. But how long some of the most far flung beers might have been there on the shelf and how likely it was that anybody would ever drink them, I couldn't really say.

They had some normal French beer on tap at the bar so we would probably have had a few of those to round off our excursion into Paris before heading back to the hotel, which was about 40km back to Marne La Vallée.

Jack – Jo

Near to where the Sima Torcy plant was – and within easy walking distance - there was a shopping centre that had a decent size supermarket and a few other places. One of these was a pizzeria cum bar and it was run by a chap who we later came to know was called Jack or "Jacky"... I think he might have originally been of Algerian origin as he had a distinctive look about him and all the pizzas had merguez on them instead of salami.

I had never tried merguez before and I really liked this variation of pizza. We went there quite often at lunchtime as it was easy to get to and made a nice change from munching on baguettes in our quiet room. In the evening, the pizza bit that opened up into the shopping centre wasn't open but the cafe bar was and they offered a nice brasserie menu for diners.

By the time I got back to Sima in the middle of January, things had evolved and our installation fitter Harry Leggatt and Jacky had become the best of bosom buddies – despite neither speaking the other's language.

As well as eating and drinking at Jacky's more often, we also occasionally socialised with him – and his highly decorative blonde girlfriend Christine - in the evenings.

One evening we went to a very swish restaurant in the centre of Paris called L'Univers. I'm not sure if it is there any more as I can't find it mentioned anywhere on the internet - and other places with a similar name don't look anything like this one.

It was quite hairy trying to negotiate our way through the busy streets of central Paris in the dark in three separate cars – without getting anybody lost.

This was back in the days before everybody had mobile phones, of course, but because they were often away on installations together, a lot of the Field Engineers had CB radios in their cars so that they could communicate with each other.

So we had Harry Leggatt, Jack and Christine up in front leading the way, Graham Perkins, Chris Rojek and me behind them and Mark Leaning – and whoever else was in his car - someway behind. Graham was driving and trying his best to keep up with Harry and Jack and not get lost and I was relaying directions to Mark over the radio – which was all quite fun, looking back at it now.

Jacky - being rather unhelpful through all of this - kept picking up Harry's radio and saying silly things like "Wal –Kie Tal-Kie - Hello!" and singing an appalling French accented rendition of Dean Martin's "Everybody Loves Somebody" over the air at us...

Anyway, we eventually got there, got parked and congregated outside the impressive restaurant building.

L'Univers was a sumptuous place with heavy elaborate curtains all round, gold everywhere and crystal lighting throughout. We were in a large ornate upstairs room and there were lots of very smart people there.

One guy who was at a neighbouring table was pointed out to us. He was oldish and a bit scruffy and sitting with two dolly birds. We were told in hushed tones that he was a prominent "artiste trottoir" – ie: a pavement artist, which I assume, in his case, meant something a little more than those people who chalk on paving stones...

I initially misunderstood the description and thought he was eloquently referring to the girls as being tarts... but there you go. The rich tapestry of language!

*****

On another evening, Jack took us to an authentic North African cous cous restaurant - also in Paris.

Now, this was in some odd gloomy suburb to the north of the city around St Denis and was the sort of the area place that you would never go to on your own and, if you did stumble upon it by accident, you'd get the hell out of there as quickly as you could!

The restaurant was on a dimly lit back street and, compared to L'Univers, didn't look particularly inviting from the outside. Even inside it wasn't much of a palace and looked more like a take away with a few tables wedged in. There were no table cloths - just heavily marked Formica tops - and basic plastic chairs to sit on. There was also the obligatory French cafe pinball machine in one corner.

Barring a couple of staff, there was nobody in there at all and nobody else came in during the whole time we were there. To be honest, I got the distinct impression that Jacky had got them to open up especially for our benefit.

He may even have owned the place for all I knew – but, if he did, he certainly didn't make a big thing of it.

Awful though the place was, the food was absolutely wonderful. I had never actually seen cous cous before and had missed out on having it at a social evening at Isabel's house in Montpellier back in 1984 when I wasn't able to get there until later, so this was the first time I got to see it and taste it.

The food was brought out on huge platters piled up with meats and loads of exotic vegetables that I had never tried before. There were endless carafes of some unnamed red wine - and bottles of French beer for those who preferred that.

It really was an unforgettable experience – both from the point of view of the strange venue and the delicious food - and Jack was a really welcoming and generous host.

*****

I had a weekend at home halfway through my second stint at Sima so that would have been in mid to late February. I spent the Monday morning in the office catching up on things, took the train down to the airport in the afternoon, and got the early evening flight back to Paris.

Mark Leaning picked me up at the airport and said that we had to go straight to Jack's bar as it was his birthday and he was having a party.

That was the last thing that I fancied doing getting straight off the plane after a long day but I had little choice but to go along. Luckily, it wasn't really "that kind of party" and there were only we Baker Perkins personnel there, along with Jacky and Christine.

They had gone to a lot of trouble and there was a huge expensive looking buffet laid out across the tables with red and black caviar (the only time I have ever had that, by the way) flutes of champagne and all sorts of other delicacies that I can't even remember now.

Having said that there was only us there – that was not quite true. There were three or four swarthy types (to use a rather outdated expression) who had dark hair and were wearing heavy black leather jackets – even though it was quite warm indoors.

The "modern me" would immediately leap to describe them as looking like criminals out of an episode of "Engrenages". Luckily I didn't know too much about the Parisian underworld in those days, so that thought didn't spring to mind.

I couldn't work out whether they had actually been invited to the party – or whether they had just seen the lights on in the bar and come in as it was open – and that Jacky didn't want to turn them away.

He certainly didn't seem to be over pally with them and spent most of the evening talking to us.

Later on they did come over and start mixing with us – which made me feel rather uncomfortable. One guy kept going around telling everybody that he was a Gypsy (Gitan) and that he had a Mercedes.

Mark Leaning was chatting away to him in his basic "learned by ear" conversational French that he had picked up on various installations over the years in France and was humouring him saying things like "Tray bon, missuer.."

By this time of the evening, I was feeling rather grotty having over-eaten on the nibbles and had some champagne despite not really wanting any – plus being exhausted from the flight - so I was not really at my most sociable.

And I was really not in the least bit interested in this bloke's background or what sort of car he drove. And I did something that I have never done before or since in the presence of French speaking people. I called this adult male, who was not known to me, "tu" instead of "vous".

That may not sound like very much but, in terms of the diplomacy and politesse that goes hand in hand with the French language, that was an EXTREMELY impolite thing to do - and it inferred that I felt dismissive of him, which I probably meant to at the time as I wasn't in the mood for chit chat.

Luckily, he didn't seem to pick up on this, probably thought I was some damned foreigner that couldn't speak French properly and, instead, just wandered off to bug somebody else.

While all this was going on, I also had to contend in the background with Sticks being the harbinger of doom and gloom and muttering to anybody who was listening "There's going to be trouble here... It always ends up with fights at the end of the night with the gypsies back home..."

Luckily, the mysterious guests didn't stay for very much longer and - contrary to Sticks' well-voiced concerns - they weren't waiting to beat us up in the car park when we left either.

Sunday Afternoon with Tony's Sister in Rosny.

Over time, I have become used to bizarre experiences - but one of the most unlikely things I had ever known came on a Sunday afternoon during a quiet period on the Sima installation early in 1989.

Tony Santoro had mentioned his sister in passing on a few occasions and it turned out that she actually lived on the outskirts of Paris, not very far – in the general scheme of things - from where we were based.

We had gone into the Sima factory on this particular Sunday morning but nothing much was due to happen so Tony announced that he was going to go and visit his sister and would I like to go along?

Now, Tony – and his sister - were "Peterborough Italians". Just to explain - that means that their parents came over from Italy – presumably in the 1950s, like a great many others - to find work in the brickyards and other associated industries in the area who were at the time crying out for unskilled labour - as there was little chance of gainful employment in the south of Italy.

Much of the local brick industry was situated around the Fletton area of Peterborough during this period and many Italian families settled there.

They then had children here who went to local schools and they, in turn, have since had their own children and, over time, a huge Italian community has grown up around the city.

My school fell inside the catchment area for a lot of people from Fletton and, because the parents of the English-born children wanted them to learn "proper" Italian – rather than just the various regional dialects that were spoken informally at home - that is why Italian was taught as a second foreign language after French at our school.

And, as I had an aptitude for languages (or was useless at anything else – however you prefer to look at it...), that is how I came to study O level and A level Italian.

Now, I had never met Tony before we both travelled out for the Sima installation - and I had never met his sister before either - so I imagine that the main reason he asked ME to go with him was so that I could help out if he got into any linguistic difficulties on the way.

Anyway, it was very kind of him and I readily agreed as a nice trip out to the Paris suburbs would be infinitely more enjoyable than hanging around the factory all day with nothing to do.

As it was a Sunday morning, the offices were all empty and the reception was closed. There was no Sandrine to ask to ring up and order a taxi and I hadn't a clue how the phone system worked or who I ought to ask.

All of a sudden, Monsieur Coty appeared. He had apparently popped into the plant to do some maintenance job earlier that morning while it was quiet and when I asked him how we could get hold of a taxi, he kindly offered to drive Tony and me to the railway station himself.

He dropped us off at the Marne La Valée RER station (that stands for Réseau Express Régional - Regional Express Network in English – and links the underground Metro system with the commuter suburbs).

I had never been on the RER before so it was an interesting experience for me, albeit being pretty much the same as any other train you might ever have been on - and with it being Sunday and there being no commuters about, the journey didn't take very long.

Plus it was nice to see the area in daylight for a change – even though it was a gloomy winter's day.

We got off the RER at Rosny Sous Bois and I suddenly discovered (at this rather late point in our journey) that Tony wasn't 100% sure where we were going! He didn't know the address – which meant that we couldn't ask anybody for directions – and he didn't appear to have his sister's phone number with him either, so we couldn't even call her and ask to be rescued.

After the best part of an hour or so of tramping round some pleasant leafy French suburbs – all of which looked exactly the same to me, and during which time I had completely lost all track of how to get back to the RER station - we came across a building that Tony thought looked "kind of familiar".

I wasn't overly reassured by this but he went and rang the bell and the door was opened by a pleasant blondish lady who smiled and said, in an unmistakably Peterborough-type accent:

"Ah - You found it all right, then!". So we had successfully arrived.

Tony's sister was called Rosa and she was married to an Italian called Paolo Marseglia – I'm not sure where he was originally from - and they were both pleased to see us and very welcoming.

Rosa had been preparing a big meal for us – so the visit had obviously not been quite so haphazardly arranged as it had seemed to me. So we sat round the table and enjoyed this sumptuous Sunday lunch – accompanied by plenty of wine. After the meal we all sat in the lounge sipping on Grappa – which I had never tried before – and generally chatting.

Rosa spoke to Tony and me in English but Paolo didn't appear to know any English and she spoke to him in French.

The husband and I conversed in French but Tony, not knowing any French, spoke to him in Italian. So it was all rather confusing - to say the least, especially when you are comfortably full up and dozy after a nice meal and a load of wine.

Coming back now to what I mentioned earlier about regional dialects and the Italian post-war diaspora, Tony spoke to his brother in law in standardised Italian and not in the dialect that he - and his sister - would have learnt at home as his parents' mother tongue.

Whether this was a "politeness" thing – or whether he had come from a different region and therefore might not have understood the Santoro family dialect, I am not really sure - but it was all rather fascinating.

What I did notice, however – and I mean no disrespect here whatsoever – was that Tony's spoken standardised Italian was rather awkward...

But this meant that I could immediately recognise first-hand what it was that the Fletton parents wanted to achieve by getting their children to learn proper Italian and proper grammar at school. They wanted to be sure that if they went back to live in Italy, they would be able to communicate on an equal basis with everybody else and not be limited within their own community of origin.

So it was an interesting experience on many different levels.

It was pretty dark and cold and horrible when we were ready to go back to the Novotel and, while Tony and I were perfectly content to go back the way we had come, Rosa and her husband were worried about the frequency of trains on a Sunday evening and they kindly drove us all the way back instead.

More Top 50, M6 – and Frank Bruno!

I mentioned the Top 50 TV show that used to be Canal+ on weekdays when we were at the installation at IGPM. We still had the Top 50 show on at tea time while getting ready to meet up for the evening and, once again I got into a lot of the French music that was popular at the time.

In fact, by the time I went to Sima in October 1988, a new channel had also been launched on French TV called M6. In the mornings when we were getting up and getting ready to go down to breakfast, M6 used to show back to back music videos (a bit like MTV but with no waffle in between) so this was another great way of getting to hear more French hits of the day.

One of my favourite songs from that period was "Jour de Neige" by Elsa (full name Elsa Lunghini – she is a cousin, by the way, to the gorgeous Joséphine Jobert, who plays Florence Cassel in the BBC's Death In Paradise...) .

The song was released in November 1988 and was flying high in the charts in the early part of 1989. I bought Elsa's eponymous debut album off the back of it and that has lots of lovely songs on it.

The big number one in France when I went back to Sima in January 1989 was "High" by David Hallyday – son of the famous French rock n roller Johnny Hallyday. It remained at number one for the whole of January and into the first week of February.

Then it was replaced at the top of the charts by "Pour Toi Armenie" which was a charity ensemble record put together by French national treasure Charles Aznavour in response to a catastrophic earthquake that had occurred in the country of his birth in December 1988.

The song featured numerous French singers and personalities recorded in a similar style to Band Aid's "Feed the World" and it stayed at number one for 10 weeks until the middle of April.

According to Wikipedia, it was the first ever song to enter the French charts straight at number one.

A few other songs that I fondly remember from that time include:

"Amor De Mis Amores" by Paco, which was sung wholly in Spanish

"Sketch of Love" by Thierry Mutin, which was based on the haunting tune to Händels' "Sarabande"

And "La Fête Au Village" which was a fun party song by Les Musclés.

On Saturday 25th February we all stopped up late to watch Frank Bruno take on Mike Tyson in Las Vegas for the world heavyweight boxing championship. The French TV rights to the fight belonged to Canal+ which showed the fight live at some ridiculous time in the early hours of the morning.

The TVs in our hotel rooms only had the basic free version of Canal+ which meant that we could see the encrypted version of the fight.

This consisted of the picture flashing on and off at 10 second intervals and the picture - when it was there – being interrupted by hazy lines streaming across it.

The audio worked ok, though, so there was constant commentary and, if you'd had a few drinks, and kept your eyes squinted, you could make out most of what was going on.

Luckily, the fight only lasted 5 rounds before it was awarded to Tyson on a technical knockout and we were all finally able to go to sleep!

Arcade Afternoon

Baker Perkins used to use firms of subcontractors to do much of their electrical wiring and pipework on installation sites. The reason for that was, with things becoming more specialised over time, there was not necessarily enough work all year round - certainly not on the same continent - to have a full crew of electricians and plumbers employed all the time.

So they used firms like AL Electrics who did all the electrical wiring and Arcade who did the water and oil plumbing and, over time, those companies had built up as good an understanding of the requirements of our products as the BP engineers had.

It was up to the individual customer which company they employed to do their own piping and electrical work, and they were provided well in advance with a detailed set of "services drawings" which showed at what points on the press these had to be laid to.

But it was always useful if they used the same company that we did as it made everything much easier to co-ordinate and we could be sure that the connections between the two areas of responsibility all worked properly.

So, as part of the initial contract phase of the job, our engineers would "suggest" that the customer might like to look at AL Electrics and Arcade to do their side of the work for them – but it was ultimately up to them.

While I was at Sima, preparations were well under way for the next press installation which was to be a G16 at Roto France Impression (RFI) which was in the same area.

Although I had never been there, I knew their Technical Directeur Jaques Pille as I had met him when he had made a previous visit to Peterborough and I seem to think that Anne and I took him the Grain Barge – that's an expensive floating Chinese restaurant on a boat on the River Nene - for a meal once as well.

Anyway, Chris West from Arcade was over in Marne La Vallée checking on the progress of the final pipe connections at Sima and he had arranged to go to see M. Pille and make a pitch for doing the customer pipework for the RFI installation.

As we were "keen" for his company to get the contract, it was suggested that I might go along with him and help with communications at the meeting. So, off we went one afternoon to deliver a sales presentation about Arcade's plumbing services and the amount of experience that they'd had on installations of Baker Perkins presses.

Now, I had no personal experience of the plumbing and pipework side of the installation and no specialised French terminology stored up in my brain for that particular "métier" so I really wasn't sure how this was going to go.

Luckily, it all worked out very well as Chris spoke no French at all and was over the moon to basically have the chance to be able to get his message across – and all the presentation materials and piping drawings were sufficiently clear for Pille to be able to understand without me having to go into too much technical detail.

Chris was so pleased with how the meeting had gone that he wanted to pay me for my time, but as I was still on the clock for Baker Perkins for the afternoon, I thought that it would be immoral of me and I refused to accept it.

He then said that he had actually wanted to take us all out for a meal that evening anyway but now had to fly back to England – so, instead, he pressed the same roll of French Francs into my hand and told me to treat the lads on his behalf. So honour was served on both sides!

Once I got back to England properly, Chris asked me to translate his quote for RFI into French for him – as a private "after work" job - which I happily did, and I did allow him to pay me for doing that.

I never got to visit the Roto France installation so I don't know what came of my sales presentation endeavours that day - and I was never contacted to translate a quotation for the subsequent Avenir Graphique installation, so I guess he must have re-used my RFI text and merely put new figures on it...!

French Safety Inspector

One matter that took up quite a lot of my time in my last few weeks at Sima was dealing with the local Health & Safety Inspector.

We had come up against problems with the Safety Inspector at IGPM – not while I was there but when he had been called in later to give the machine its safety certificate. I ended up having to translate a long 5 or 6 page report that he had produced where he had called for several major enhancements to be added along with loads of other footling minor things.

So we had to work through all this with the mechanical and electrical engineering departments in Peterborough and come up with solutions that were acceptable to the Inspector.

But, at least it meant that we had all the French safety measures already in place for the installation at Sima so there wouldn't be a problem with the safety inspection – or so we thought.

However, it turned out that Marne La Vallée was in a different region to St Etienne and not only did they have different regional safety inspectorate offices, they also had DIFFERENT SAFETY REGULATIONS.

Whereas the IGPM inspector had made us mount additional safety stop buttons all over the place (a perfectly reasonable safety feature – just not very aesthetic being stuck willy nilly on the otherwise smooth lines of the machine) this guy in Marne La Valleé had a thing about narrow access areas and trailing electrical wires - so we had people following him around with packets of cable ties fixing things in place.

M Coty had been moaning to me about the general cabling that we had used for the electrical wiring as he said that the HT cables that ran above the factory could cause interference and the wiring needed to be more shielded than it was.

When the inspector turned up at the Sima installation, M Coty started buttonholing him and drawing his attention to various things on the press that he thought he ought to look at.

I thought he ought to just leave the guy to get on with his job and after a while I got a bit fed up with this.

I got hold of Joseph LeTurluer, who was an engineer from our Paris agents OFMAG and was with us doing extra bits and pieces around the G14 installation, and told him to stick with the Inspector all the time he was there and keep an ear open for what M Coty was saying to him in case he was trouble-making.

Funnily enough, one of the Sima printers who had overheard me talking to Joseph came over afterwards, slapped me on the shoulder and said what a sensible idea it was to put Joseph on the case...

Joseph, by the way, had been the maintenance engineer at Sigma Prim in Châtelaudren, near St Brieuc in Brittany, where we had installed a G14 press in 1986.

The printers there had gone bust and the press was eventually repossessed and Joseph ended up working as a trouble-shooter for OFMAG. He had previously been an engineer on oil tankers, had travelled round the world several times and was a very pleasant chap.

I met him a few more times later on when he came to visit the Peterborough factory and always got on well with him.

So I had a hair-pulling few days sending faxes back and forth to the engineers in Peterborough discussing the trials and tribulations about the constantly changing safety requirements and, as a result of my various deliberations with the Inspector at Sima – and with two more press installations coming up in the same region at Roto France Impression and Avenir Graphique, I actually became our company French safety "expert" for a short while – despite having no engineering background or safety training.

The electrical engineers regularly consulted me on how many extra stop buttons were needed and where they needed to go and, with the RFI press being a G16 press and having taller print units, they needed more stop buttons than a G14.

Zeroing The Ink Keys

One of the most time consuming – but essential - jobs prior to being able to get the print units ready to go was setting up the inking system – or to be more specific, zeroing the ink keys.

Back in the old days, this had to be done by hand but I imagine that if the same type of system is still being used today, it will all now be done via computer.

To understand what I am talking about here, it is worth spending a few minutes looking at how the inking system works and how the ink gets onto the paper.

Don't forget, I am not a professional engineer or a trained printer, this is not a full and formal technical explanation, it's just what I have picked up over the time I was involved in presses with Baker Perkins / Rockwell.

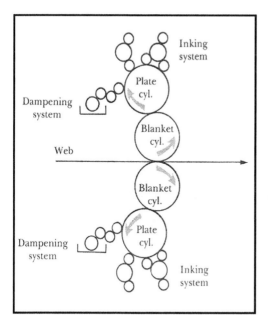

This is a diagram of the cylinder and roller configuration of a Baker Perkins print unit.

You can find lots more fascinating information like this on the Baker Perkins Historical Society website at www.bphs.net/ historyofkeybusinesses/ printing/index.html

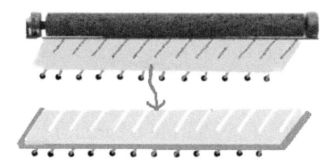

This isn't actually a Baker Perkins 26 key segmented ink duct blade but it does at least gives a rough idea of a similar duct blade with adjustable ink keys. (Source: https://printing.santhipriya.com)

The ink gets put into the ink duct and, as you can see from the configuration diagram on the previous page, everything is mirrored on a G14 / G16 print unit - recto & verso - so as to print on both sides of the paper at the same time.

So if it is the black print unit, you have black ink both top and bottom, red ink in the red unit and so on...

Across the outlet of the ink duct is a segmented ink duct blade, made of stainless steel, which controls how much ink is allowed onto the ink rollers.

This has very fine laser cut slits right across its length to divide it into segments – 26 in the case of a Baker Perkins G14 press in the late 1980s.

Each of these segments across the width of the unit is adjusted by an "ink key" which isn't actually a "key" at all but a screw that opens and closes the gap between the blade segment and the ink roller according to what you want to do with it. In fact, to avoid any confusion, the ink keys are actually called ink screws in French – "vis d'encrier".

Now, the actual amount of ink applied to the paper during printing to achieve the colours required is adjusted remotely from the control desk but, in order for that to work accurately, it has to start off from a recognisable reference point – and that is the ink key zero.

That doesn't literally mean that the ink keys allow zero ink out, but it is at least a "zero point" as far as the colour control system is concerned and what the printers had to do was go along and set every ink key on every ink duct on every print unit   (that's 26 x 2 x 4= 208 in total), by hand so that they had a common zero point across the machine.

Luckily, once I had helped Graham Perkins, our printer for the start up, explain what the Sima printers needed to do - and he had watched them do a couple of ink keys to make sure they were doing it right – I had no further involvement with this time consuming exercise – but it is a fascinating thing to know about...

Back in the days I am talking about here, a Baker Perkins press had an "Instacolour" system that allowed you to adjust the colours remotely once your copies were being printed.

The Instacolour system had a control screen that allowed you to select which colour station you wanted to adjust and there was a "layout desk" ie a big flat surface where you could lay your printed copy out to examine it.

I have mentioned before that all the colours of the rainbow are basically obtained from a mixture of black, cyan, magenta and yellow, so there were 26 buttons across the bottom of the layout desk – which corresponded to the 26 ink keys across the ink duct.

You'd do that for each of the 4 colours as required and you'd then turn the sheet over and do the same for the other side so that all 4 print units were printing at the desired quality, recto & verso.

So, if your green was a bit off, you'd need to adjust the inking on the blue or yellow units – and so on...

What you would do is you'd have a layout desk which was the correct size to hold an unfolded copy – ie 630mm height by 965mm width at Sima. You'd lay your printed copy out on this desk and look at the image quality and you could then increase the density of whatever colour needed it by using the 26 control buttons beneath the copy which related to the ink duct keys.

As An Example - say you wanted to print an image of the French flag across the full width of your paper web.

Not that you would actually do that in reality as, once it had been cut to length and gone through the folding process, you'd end up with a 16-page folded magazine with 1/8 of a French flag on each page, which wouldn't really be very interesting.

But, as the French flag has clearly defined areas of colour, we can certainly use this as an example of how the inking coverage on the print units might work.

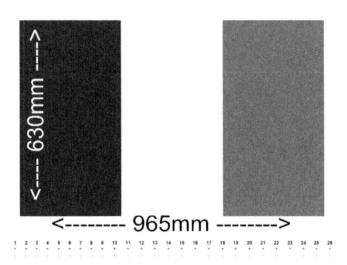

A simplified example of how the flat printed signature would look when placed on the layout desk. The control buttons for the 26 ink keys are along the bottom.

Unit 2: Cyan / Recto

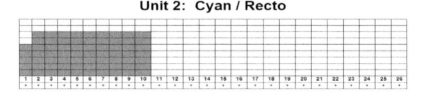

The inking profile for the blue print unit for the French flag would show up something like this (above) on the control screen of the colour control system – and you would be able to bring up separate screens on the monitor to set up the upper and lower inking systems for each individual print unit.

In order to get the shade of blue right, you would compare the signature that you have just printed off, with the master copy to see what the requirements are and adjust the setting of the ink keys that control the ink flow onto the area of the blue colouring – in this case keys 1 to 10 – accordingly.

If you wanted to make the blue colour darker, you might introduce some black ink from the black printing unit into the image and that would be applied by modifying the settings of ink keys 1 to 10 on the black unit.

If, when you had finished your print run of French flags, you wanted to do a run of Italian flags, you would apply yellow ink from the yellow print unit to the mix with the blue and adjust both colours until you got the correct shade of green.

Now, while the no1 printer was doing that, and getting the printed image right, another one of his crew would be working on the folder settings and making minute adjustments so that the cut to length and the tabloid and quarter fold were falling in the right place on the finished copy.

As I mentioned before, I am not very good with folders and, because the C2 folder that was being supplied with the new G14 press at Sima was very similar in terms of operation and adjustment to the existing C2 folder that they had on their old G16, the operators didn't really need much instruction on how to use it. That being the case, I had very little involvement in interpreting on the folder setup and settings – hence my comparative ignorance in that department!

So, once the image quality was perfect and the folder settings correct, the conveyor taking the finished copies off the folder delivery would be diverted to the stacker - and away from the waste skip – the press would be brought up to full speed and the copy count would be switched on – and that's basically how a printing press works!

So there you go. That's more or less the story of how the Baker Perkins G14 press was installed at Sima Torcy in Marne La Vallée during the period October 1988 to March 1989.

I wasn't there for the whole time, of course - and I haven't gone into the minutest detail about every little thing that happened - but I was there when the first equipment was delivered.

And the press was running properly and printing in full colour by the time that I left, so I look upon that period - and the help that I was able to give - with a feeling of great satisfaction.

1990: French Visitors – Avenir Graphique

For much of 1990, I seemed to be involved with helping with the training courses for printers and engineers from Avenir Graphique in Marne La Vallée who had ordered 3 three Baker Perkins G14 presses.

I seem to think there were 4 or 5 groups who came over in total - so that's actually only 4 or 5 weeks out of 52, but it was a disproportionately long time to be involved with something that wasn't my actual job!

The first group came over in December 1989 and I can narrow this down to the first week in December because Steve Kimber and I had to go and pick them up from Leeds / Bradford Airport (apparently, the flights were cheaper to fly there than to Heathrow or Stansted) and I clearly remember on the car radio all the fuss about the new Band Aid 2 version of "Do They Know It's Christmas" which had been recorded using new popular artists such as Kylie Minogue, Jason Donovan and Bros.

It was a really cold horrible gloomy day and it snowed on the way up but the flight arrived safely and we took the visitors off for a pub lunch before driving back to Peterborough.

This first group had the chief engineer Michel Vallinot and the production manager –whose name I have forgotten (sorry...!) – and they came over for the first course to get an idea of what was involved and, during the spring and summer of 1990, the main training groups came afterwards.

I'm afraid it's all a bit of a haze for me who did what and when and, over time, this whole period had merged into one soggy gloop of vague memories.

So, rather than trying to give you chapter and verse of a load of facts that are probably no longer relevant, I will just give you a few general reminiscences and funny incidents.

As I may have mentioned before, the training courses that we held at Baker Perkins were for the main part, extra sweeteners that we offered to customers who were buying a new press – although they were also available to anybody as a chargeable item.

The training manager was Roger Davis and he delivered all the courses, with the option of bringing in a particular engineer from the mechanical, electrical or installation side if a particular issue needed to be addressed.

The courses were mainly classroom based and the students were guided through the operating manuals for their new press equipment, talked through layout drawings and electrical schematics and could ask any questions that arose.

These sessions were fairly relaxed and fun – and there was plenty of coffee and breaks in between sessions.

The students were also taken to the factory floor where they could see their press equipment being assembled and this gave them the chance to see the individual components being finished off and mounted on the units and folders.

Seeing how something is actually built is a good way of understanding why it might go wrong in the future so I always thought this was a very useful part of the training visit, and we often went back to the fitting shop a number of times over the week so they could see the progression of the assembly works.

There was also the option of a quick jaunt to the nearby Bretton factory where all the electronic control desks were manufactured - along with visits to see existing customers' presses in operation.

Now, as I have also touched on previously, I have no technical background and am not a trained printer so my role in these training courses was purely to interpret what was being said to make sure that the French visitors got the most out of it.

I wasn't even a proper trained interpreter (and still am not...) and, back at that time, I hadn't even studied languages at University.

My role as the French "expert" for the company just evolved over time with the various experiences that I had been lucky enough to have and I just happened to be in the right place at the right time!

Now, before we go any further, here are:

A Few Words About Interpreting.

In the professional world of interpreting, there are three main types of interpreting: Simultaneous, Consecutive and Liaison.

Simultaneous Interpreting.

Simultaneous is what they do at conferences and the United Nations - and other such places - where somebody sits in a booth, listens to what the speaker is saying and puts that into the language of the listener – pretty much simultaneously, which is why it is so called.

It is very difficult to do as you have to be closely listening out for the next bit in the speaker's language at the same time as you are saying the previous bit in the listener's language. They speak at normal speed and they don't go back just because you have missed a bit, so it is a high pressure situation.

You have to get it word perfect and accurate first time otherwise wars could break out as a result. And there's me agonising about what to call a particular tool in French...!

As I have said before, professional simultaneous interpreters have regular breaks and tend to burn out before they get to a great age, and can't do it anymore. But they do get paid a lot!

I have never actually done Simultaneous Interpreting in a formal setting. It's a professional skill that I have never learnt.

What I may have done occasionally is whisper out of the corner of my mouth to whoever I may be with what the speaker is talking about - and possibly highlight any crucial points that might need explaining.

Rather like if you are explaining to somebody what is happening in a television programme where they have missed the beginning.

Consecutive Interpreting.

Consecutive Interpreting – which I did a bit of during my later University studies - is where the speaker says a sentence, you put that into the listener's language and then the speaker says another sentence.

This is a bit easier as you get the time to fully listen to the source wording and then think about the translation before moving onto the next bit.

It is less pressured and more time can be taken over it. This sort of interpreting is what you'd probably come across in a classroom situation or possibly when showing a group of visitors around a building or an attraction.

Liaison Interpreting.

This is where you are acting as a communication link in a conversation between two people. It is very similar to Consecutive Interpretation in so far as you would listen to the first sentence, interpret that and then move onto the next one.

The difference here is that you are translating in both directions – ie both from and into each person's language at the same time - and switching depending on who is speaking.

Now, in all three of the above cases, when you are acting as an interpreter, you do not have any input into the conversation yourself as a person. You are merely acting as a voice for the speaker.

If he says: "I would like to offer you a drink", you say exactly that in French – or whatever language you are using.

If you "explain" what he or she said - rather than interpret - and you say "He wants to offer you a drink", that is not correct interpreting, but it all really depends on the situation, who the various parties are and what is required.

Now I have to say – and sack me if you wish, although it is a bit late for that now ... - that all the time I was helping out on press installations - or customer visits - or training courses with Baker Perkins, I never actually engaged in formal interpreting in the truly correct sense of the term.

I have never been professionally trained as a proper interpreter so I never got into the habit of the detached impersonal way of interacting between speaker and listener as I have described above.

I never actually saw myself as an objective intermediary because I was there on behalf of our company as a company employee. In short, I was one of "us", they were "them" - and I was there to help us to communicate with them.

For example, if we were in a restaurant and Graham Perkins said "Can I see the wine list, please?", I would not interpret that word for word in the first person for the benefit of the waiter, I would just say "We'd like to see the wine list."

Now, because I knew a lot about the press machinery and had been involved in two recent press installations, this gave me a big advantage over any random interpreter who might otherwise be called in to assist with language communication.

When I was helping with these training courses at Peterborough for the engineers and printers from Avenir Graphique during 1990, the main course content was pretty similar from week to week so I got to know it all by heart. Plus, I also understood and could readily answer myself most of the questions that the engineers might have.

So what tended to happen was that Roger Davis – the trainer / tutor – would say something. I would interpret what he had said – and then quite often chip in with something extra which I thought might help their understanding - or that I knew from my own experience was also relevant to the question.

That would lead to a follow up question and we would end up having a highly animated and detailed discussion in French - going off at a complete tangent to the original thing that Roger was talking about.

On more than one occasion, he had to wave at me and remind me that HE was the one who was supposed to be running the class – but he took it all in good humour, of course, and then we would get back on track.

*****

We generally had sandwich lunches during the day in the training room but on the Friday, Roger tended to take the visitors out for lunch somewhere for a change and to give them a taste of English culture.

One very nice day I remember we went to The Green Man at Marholm – which is actually officially called The Fitzwilliam Arms but everybody knows it as the Green Man because of an ancient adjacent privet hedge. That was a warm sunny day and we sat outside and ate in the beer garden.

On another occasion we went to the carvery at the Gordon Arms and there we had a bit of a clash between French and English cultures.

As is normal practice at a lot of these places, the very pleasant waitress came round with the bread basket and asked if we would like a white or brown roll.

We English guys said what we wanted and were duly served - but the French guys couldn't see the point of the question, even though I was doing my very best interpreting act.

In most typical restaurants in France, they automatically bring out a whole basket of bread and leave it on the table for the duration of the meal. Using a chunk of baguette to wipe the remaining sauce off your plate is an integral part of a French meal and our visitors couldn't understand why they were being limited to one measly bread roll each.

In a brave attempt to resolve this situation, I took the pleasant waitress over to one side and explained that, with our guests being French, they were used to having a basket of bread on the table and if she could leave the whole thing there for us, that would be super.

This seemed to cause quite a problem and I wasn't really sure whether they were worried about the extra cost of a few bread rolls or if they only actually had one bread basket for the whole restaurant but, as they was nobody else dining at that point anyway, the girl reluctantly agreed to leave the bread on the table.

Another moment of hilarity occurred when the same waitress came round with a tray of condiments – here again, one sachet each was the going rate.

When somebody asked for Mustard – she enquired "French or English?"

This again caused a lot of consternation around the table – especially as the French Mustard that was served up didn't resemble in the least what the average French person thought of as being mustard - and they all decided that they preferred the English to the French on this occasion.

I don't actually like mustard so have very little to say on this matter but the website www.frenchconnexion.com describes the differences between the various types of mustard as follows:

MENTION the phrase "French mustard" to the average Briton and they will think of the mild, dark brown kind that was popularised by the Norwich-based firm Colman's.

However to most French people this is a mystery - one French blogger described it as "that sweet English stuff they have the nerve to call 'French Mustard'."

In fact the nearest real French equivalent - called moutarde brune - or sometimes moutarde de Bordeaux - is not very common in France where the best-known mustard is Dijon, especially as sold by market leader Amora Maille.

British-style "French mustard" would also be classed as a "moutarde douce" - a term used for certain sweeter, milder mustards in France.

Dijon is a dark yellow, with a milder taste than English mustard, but still with more bite and a more classic mustard taste than the sweetish, savoury, "French mustard".

Another task that we had to perform, which was OK in small doses but, after about 4 or 5 weeks became a bit of a chore, was taking the visiting engineers out in the evenings.

We had started using the Queensgate Hotel on Fletton Avenue (near to the traffic lights with London Road near The Peacock pub and football ground) to accommodate visiting engineers as it was a bit cheaper than the Bull Hotel in the town centre for "non-chargeable" courses – and was also easier to get to and from.

Upon arrival at the hotel and having briefly explored the surrounding area, one group of engineers decided that they wanted to go and eat at the nearby Kentucky Fried Chicken place. I didn't fancy this at all as I'd had a "bad experience" associated with a different KFC joint in the past (other food outlets are available – and I have been ill after going to some of those as well...).

So, with the customer always being right, off we went to KFC and, to be fair to all concerned, everybody seemed to enjoy themselves and I even had a bite to eat as well.

On another occasion, a different group decided that they wanted to go to Deep Pan Pizza in town and that was fine by me as I was a big fan of Deep Pan Pizza and always liked their food.

We got in and got seated and I ran through the menu for everybody. Having seen the nice welcoming healthy salad bar on the way in, they all decided they'd like a mixed salad to start off with.

Here again, we had the clash of cultures when the waitress came round and gave them a tiny little "side salad" bowl each.

Don't forget, this was back in 1990 before many of the healthy eating campaigns that we have today and, back then, a lot of people looked upon any salad items on your plate as merely decoration - so I can fully appreciate that idea of a group of big hunky men on a evening out wanting to eat piles and piles of salad would probably have been a fairly alien concept at the time.

I don't even think that a main course salad actually appeared on the menu at a lot of places at that time (that's what Americans call a "Dinner Salad" – by the way) so, once again, I had a quiet word with the waitress, told her to let the guys have whatever they wanted and we'd sort out the bill later.

In the end, I seem to think that she brought out a stack of the large main course pasta bowls and the guys were then able to go and serve themselves up a nice - suitably sized - mixed salad as a starter.

After that, they all wanted a large size pizza each – the size most people have to share – so, with the beer and mineral water sales as well, the restaurant did rather well out of our visit.

It was a very pleasant evening and I had really enjoyed it. I was just about to put the guys in a taxi to send them back to their hotel when one of them came up with the bright idea of "why don't we go to a night club?"

Now, I don't like night clubs at the best of times and never really have – although I did occasionally go along with the crowd back when I was 20 ish... - but this really didn't appeal to me at all, after a busy day and evening interpreting – and with the prospect of another day at work the next morning.

I tried telling them that a night club in England probably wasn't the same as they might be used to in France but that didn't seem to cut any mustard so I reluctantly took them to Shanghai Sam's, harbouring the vain hope that we might not get in.

However, this was Thursday night – famous back then for all the night clubs sending out free tickets to anybody who had a birthday or to get work groups to go and fill out an otherwise empty venue.

The dress restrictions were less strict on a Thursday than they were on a Friday or Saturday night and, to my great surprise, a very out of place looking middle aged guy in a sharp suit that made him look rather like a gangster, two obvious (to me, anyway...) French blokes in leather jackets and jeans – plus me in whatever I was wearing – managed to gain entry.

The night club was as "un fun" as I had expected it to be - but the guys got some drinks and went to sit down and drink in whatever atmosphere there was.

A group of what you might describe as "farmer boys" were making most of the noise and, while not wishing to sound detrimental to farmers in any way – what I mean here is a group of lads who looked as if they were from out of town – possibly from Ramsey or Warboys or Wisbech or somewhere – and looked very scruffily dressed in suits and ties that didn't really fit them properly.

I was hoping that the French visitors would quickly finish their drinks and decide that it was time to go but none of them seemed to be in a particular rush and it made me wonder what they thought was going to happen.

If they were waiting for a cabaret show to commence, they were going to be rather disappointed.

A girl was sitting in the corner on the table next to where we were and one of the French guys decided to offer to buy her a drink. In fact, worse than that, he actually wanted ME to offer to buy her a drink on his behalf.

I suggested that it might not be a good idea but he was quite insistent so, with a lot of eye rolling and sighing and apologising that I was here for work and these were some customers of mine, I made the approach.

Luckily the girl turned down the offer of the drink and I was then asked to ask her if she went to the night club often – which sounds incredibly corny in any language.

As if that wasn't bad enough, she suddenly started telling me her life story – including the fact that she was engaged to her cousin - and I quickly realised to my horror that she was with the group of Farmers Boys...

Figuring that they might not be quite as au fait with the metropolitan etiquette of nightlife as your average "towny" - and not being sure how they might react to idea of a French bloke chatting up their fiancée (or, even worse, as it probably looked to all intents and purposes as if it was ME who was chatting up said fiancée...) – I finally managed to get the French guys to agree to leave, reminding them again that they had a busy day tomorrow.

You had to cross - or go round - the dance floor to get to the exit and on the way past, another Farmer's Girl staggered towards me in a very drunken state and tried to start dancing with me.

Now, I know this sounds like the sort of thing that happens all the time to Roger Moore in an 007 film or an episode of The Saint but it wasn't really something that I was used to dealing with and I felt very uncomfortable.

In the end, I made a very "pantomimical" show of shaking my head in disbelief, sighing and extricating myself from the woman's grasp, while trying to keep up with the French guys to make sure they didn't manage to cause any more mischief.

The next morning, the French guys all looked as fresh as the proverbial daisy whereas I was completely shattered.

As luck would have it, Roger Davis wasn't in for some reason and he had arranged for the electrical installation engineer to go through the schematics with the guys. With most electrical symbols being the same the world over, this meant that I didn't have to sit in to interpret and was able to go and flop at my desk and "catch up on some paperwork".

While on the way down the corridor to get to the kettle, I came face to face with Ian McCombe who was the Personnel Director and also in overall charge of the Training Department.

He asked me how we were managing without Roger being there that day and I explained that the visitors were going through electrical drawings with James Copeland. He then asked how the week had been overall and I said it had been perfectly fine until the French guys had dragged me to a nightclub last night, which I could have done without.

Whether he was jealous at hearing about the exciting life I had been leading or what, I don't really know but the next thing that happened (although I only heard about this later...) was that he marched straight into my direct boss Deane Molyneux's office to complain that I appeared to be hung-over and needed to wake my ideas up...!

I think Deane probably appreciated that I had been run ragged over the past few weeks trying to do my own work as well as look after the French visitors so he gave me a bit of leeway and only told me about this encounter a week or so later – and he recounted it as an amusing anecdote.

*****

Another training week saw a new chief engineer come over from Sima Torcy. His name was Jean-Marie and he was an older guy who had travelled all over the world and worked in lots of different places. This meant that he spoke pretty good English and didn't need me to sit in and interpret for him.

He was booked in at the Butterfly Hotel and, as I didn't really want to leave him without French conversation for the whole of his stay, I went down and met him there the evening of his arrival and we had something to eat and talked about how the week would go.

I had a car by then so, as his hotel was more or less on my route in to work, I picked him up from the hotel each morning and took him back at the end of the day. Because I was accompanying a customer, this had the added advantage for me that I was able to use the executive car park at the front of the building for a few days instead of having to go round the back and have a longer walk like everybody else.

As the average training course day finished earlier than the normal office day, I was also able to sneak out early when he was ready to go back!

During one of our various chats, Jean-Marie told me that because of his various travels, he had developed a liking for hot spicy food so I took him to the Mumtaz Indian restaurant in Peterborough city centre one evening. He enjoyed that but said he would have preferred the spices to be a bit hotter!

Nathalie Blouin in London (above) and Hunstanton (next page), July 1990

1990: French Visitors – Nathalie Blouin

In July 1990, we had a French girl come and work in our office in Peterborough for several weeks. Her name was Nathalie Blouin and she was in – or approaching – her final year of baccalaureat at her Lycee in St Etienne.

I seem to think that she was the daughter of somebody at IGPM – or one of the other local companies that we'd had dealings with during that press installation - and that was how her visit came to be arranged.

As she was only 18, I imagine that she stayed with a family locally in Peterborough, although I wasn't involved in any of the arrangements.

Anyway, when she arrived in our office, she was "given" to Anne and myself to find useful and interesting things for her to do.

We made space for her at the end of our desk and gave her the initial task of answering our phone every time that it rang, to get her used to talking in English and recognising lots of different voices.

She had to find out who was calling and what subject they were calling about before handing the call over.

This caused a bit of consternation around the other offices for the first couple of days until people got used to the fact that we had a young French girl helping us out.

It was also a bit of a lottery as we used to get all the outside phone calls from overseas language customers routed from the main switchboard through to our phone - as well as other random external calls that they didn't know what else to do with.

We also taught Nathalie how to make tea properly – as it's impossible to get anybody in France to make a decent cup of tea – and she was schooled in operating the office photocopier and distributing mail and other documents to the other offices along our corridor.

Knowing from personal experience what it is like to be stuck on your own in a foreign country – even if you are staying with a friendly and hospitable host family – I took Nathalie under my wing and took her for a few trips out.

Under instructions from our manager Deane Molyneux, I took her to the East of England Show for the day – which was the big agricultural show that was held every year at the Showground - and one evening she came over to our house for some French nattering and to watch the England v Cameroon World Cup match on television. I daresay that they also had the match on telly at her host family's house – but what the hell...!

I took her to London for the weekend (that sounds ruder than it actually was...) – probably on the train. We used my old school friends Alan and Louise's house in Ealing as a base for our visit and camped on the floor there.

I don't really remember quite what we did now in London but I imagine that we rushed round all the sights. I do remember that we ended up on the South Bank near the Royal Festival Hall at one point, looking out across the river. That is where a famous scene with Hugh Grant and Andie Macdowell was shot for the 1994 film Four Weddings and a Funeral.

And I remember that we were at Alan and Louise's the night that England played Italy in the 3rd place play off in the World Cup. That's the game where Italy only won because England goalkeeper Peter Shilton (who was being lauded as the "best goalkeeper in the world" at the time) gave the ball away in the penalty area in a moment of distraction and let in a soft winning goal.

I also have a photo of Nathalie taken at the seaside. Now, I don't remember this at all - but I must have been there - and can only imagine that it was a day trip to Hunstanton, as that is the nearest bit of seaside to Peterborough.

That being the case, I think we must have both gone on my motorbike as I didn't have a car back then. Anyway, it looks as if the weather was warm and sunny so it will have been a nice trip.

The RGS factory at Nantes which finally closed in 2014, after many redundancies and industrial unrest over a 15 year period. (Photo source: Press Ocean)

1991: Nantes or Frankfurt?

In November 1991 I travelled to Nantes on the west coast of France.

The background to this is a bit complicated so it is probably worth explaining that first.

The company that I worked for – originally Baker Perkins PMC Ltd was acquired by the Rockwell International group – they of Space Shuttle and aviation fame, along with lots of fingers in other pies as well.

One of their pies at the time was printing machinery manufacturing and, over time, they had managed to acquire Goss in Preston who made newspaper presses, Hantscho (New York) who made magazine presses, Creusot Loire in Nantes whose old Batignolles factory originally had built railway locomotives and back in the 1960s had acquired the French rights to make and sell Halley Aller offset presses in the same way Baker Perkins had with the UK rights – and now, as I said, Baker Perkins PMC.

This basically meant that the Rockwell Graphics Systems division (RGS) could offer a printing press for every possible sector of the rotary web printing market.

Unfortunately, they weren't content with having just taken over the best company on the planet (if not the universe...) and they decided that they wanted to cut costs by economies of scale.

Somebody over in America looking at a map of Europe figured that they didn't need THREE plants (or "facilities" as they liked to call them) all doing pretty much the same thing over in Europe – and certainly not two in little old England - so one of them had to go.

With the Peterborough "facility" being closer to London - and the land therefore probably being more valuable – they decided to close that factory and move all designing, engineering and manufacturing of the Baker Perkins presses to Nantes.

So, during 1991, we had a load of French people from different departments in Nantes coming over to Peterborough as part of the handover process looking at what was what and how things were done.

One such person was Michel Foing who was the Contract Administration manager at Nantes and was responsible for the same sort of things that I was involved in doing in Peterborough.

He spotted my potential usefulness (I think he said "useFULness"...) and said that he'd like me to go over and work on PMC contracts in Nantes after the handover – which was nice.

Meanwhile, somewhere in Germany, well Frankfurt - in fact, other interesting moves were afoot.

PMC had its own dedicated sales office in Germany in Offenbach am Main, headed up by Sales Manager Michael Mandel, along with Gabriele Cordes and Inga Klemmer as office staff.

Because the German market was so important (and nigh on impossible to break in to with all the domestically made printing presses also available...), it was the only overseas territory outside of North America to have its own dedicated sales office. All the other countries were handled by local agents.

Now Rockwell Graphic Systems also had their own German sales office – in Obertshausen, not very far from Offenbach and just a bit further away from the centre of Frankfurt. And guess what! Yep – right first time. They wanted to close the PMC office down and merge it with the Obertshausen office.

I had met some of the RGS Obertshausen people at the Drupa exhibition in 1990 when we had all shared a stand together and they seemed rather pleasant.

There was – for example - Heike Heck who seemed to be the office manger and Franz Sengpiel the sales guy who spent most of his time in Eastern Europe.

Now, they also had an overall German sales director called Georg von Röhmer – who I hadn't met and he may well have been new. He managed to rub a few people up the wrong way for some reason or other but, when he came for a fact finding visit to Peterborough, he immediately spotted my talent and potential and said that he wanted me to go and work in Germany.

We had a good chat and it turned out that he wanted me to train up with Franz Sengpiel – who was headed towards retirement - and take over the sales side for the other RGS products as well as the PMC presses that i already knew about.

The package that he was offering sounded very tempting with a salary of DM 4.500 per month. I asked Gabriele how this measured up to the cost of living over there and she told me that a basic office assistant or shop worker got around DM1.500 a month at the time - and it was also 50% more than the £12k a year or so that I was getting in Peterborough the time.

I would also be given free use of the company flat – which was in the same building as the sales office - and return flights to England once a month for the first 6 months while I was settling in.

The fact that my German was rather limited at the time didn't seem to phase anybody too much as somebody of my intelligence and linguistic ability would easily pick it once I got there. So, needless to say, I rather liked the idea of all this.

But – I was still wanted in Nantes as well so thought I'd better find out as much as I could before I could properly weigh up the options.

There was a lot of coming and going between Peterborough and Nantes in the latter part of 1991 with their people coming over here and ours going over there swapping information as part of the handover.

I took advantage of this and announced that I needed to go to Nantes to check it out before I could decide whether I would want to go and live there or not.

There was an airport at Nantes and everybody else took advantage of the company's huge "money throwing around exercise" that this cost cutting handover had become by flying back and forth to cut down the journey time.

I, however, thinking ahead that if I was going to move to and live in Nantes permanently, figured that I ought to check out what it was like to drive there. So I arranged to take a company pool car for the week and booked a place on the Portsmouth to Cherbourg ferry.

I found out from Michel Carpentier – who was one of the RGS sales guys in Paris that I had met a few times – which was the best hotel to use in Nantes, got booked in there and I was all set!

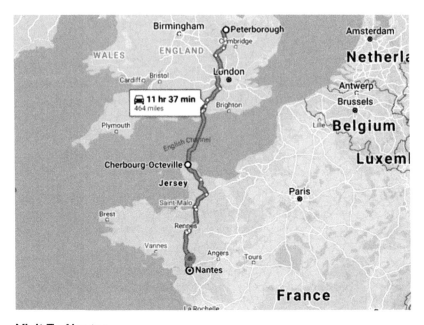

Visit To Nantes

As far as I can remember, I travelled to Nantes on the last weekend in October 1991.

I was booked on the Ferry for the Sunday morning and actually spent most of the Saturday flopping around at home with a terrible cold that had just come on. It was probably only nerves though as I felt perfectly all right the next morning.

Anne popped round on Saturday to lend me a suit carrier so that I could arrive looking all organised and executive and I set the alarm for a very early start .

It's some 550 miles from Peterborough to Nantes these days and you can travel via the tunnel which gives you more overall driving but less channel crossing time. When I went in 1991, the Tunnel hadn't opened so the only way to get there was by ferry, the best route being Portsmouth to Cherbourg.

For people with less luggage, you can also fly from London to Nantes and that only takes 1hr 20 minutes.

So the journey from Peterborough to Portsmouth was quite easy. It was early on a Sunday morning - still dark for most of the way and there was hardly any other traffic on the roads. I took the A1 / M25 / M3 and the drive took about 3 hours to do the 260 miles.

According to the internet, nowadays, the ferry crossing from Portsmouth to Cherbourg takes three hours. I seem to remember it taking longer than that but I suppose you have to get there in plenty of time beforehand. Then there's the actual getting on board and getting off on the other side. Plus the time is an hour later in France than it is here, so it would make sense that it seemed quite a lengthy undertaking.

Anyway, all went well – considering this was the first time I had ever driven myself on to a ferry and, indeed, driven myself abroad anywhere before. I didn't get sick on the boat and the weather was dry - if a bit gloomy - as I drove into France for the first time.

The route to Nantes was some 350km and it took me about 4 hours. I went past St Lô, Mt St Michel and Rennes but for the most part, it was delightful French countryside all the way as I drove through Normandy and down along the edge of Brittany.

Being a chilly late autumn Sunday afternoon, the roads were pretty empty and I was quite relieved that I was driving a well equipped and reliable car (a French Citroën no less) and had filled up to the brim with petrol before leaving England.

It was dark by the time I arrived in Nantes but I somehow managed to find my way to the hotel, get checked in and have a nice meal in the restaurant.

Exhausted after a long and eventful day, I watched French TV in my room for a while before having a good night's sleep ready for the next day.

The next morning after breakfast, I got myself spruced up in preparation for meeting new people and went off to try and find the Nantes factory.

I got parked and presented myself at reception and somebody took me through to Michel Foing's office. He was very pleased to see me and called in the other members of his contracts team to introduce me.

There was a pretty young blonde girl called Nathalie who I had seen before at Drupa but RGS had a separate reception area to us on the exhibition stand so I had never really talked to her before. There was also an older lady – by "older" here I mean older than me (I was 24 at the time) and older than Nathalie who may have been about the same – but not actually "old" as such. She was probably in her 30s – and was called Evelyne.

As far as I remember, that was the whole of the office staff for the contract administration department and that was who I would be working with. They didn't have a secretary – they did all their typing themselves and had a very modern (for the time) Wang word processing system that allowed them to share documents between offices, way before most places had ever heard of emails and internet.

I had a guided tour around the offices and the factory. Don't ask me what it was like – once you have been around a few offices and factories they are all pretty much the same.

In the evening Nathalie picked me up from the hotel and we met Michel and Evelyne in a nice restaurant somewhere in town. The following evening I just went out with the girls.

Everybody at Nantes was very pleasant and I liked the place in general. Despite it being the end of October, the weather was very pleasantly warm and, as Nantes is sort of halfway between the Brittany peninsular and Bordeaux down the west coast, I imagine it would be very nice in summer.

Nantes was inland on the banks of the River Loire but just 60km to the coast so within an easy drive for a nice day out. They had a good football team and even an ice rink and ice hockey teams so it would really have been a good place for me to move to.

On my last full day in Nantes (I can't remember now if it was the Wednesday or the Thursday...) I met the top man. I am not going to name him here as it's not fair but I really didn't take to him at all.

Having said that, I never felt wholly comfortable in the presence of Ian Mackay either – with his bombastic personality - but I had already been working at Baker Perkins for 2½ years before I ever got round to meeting him so that was a different situation all together.

I mentioned what the German office had been offering me in terms of incentives to move to Obertshausen and he didn't seem overly moved by any of it. He certainly didn't seem to be singing from the same hymn sheet as Michel Foing and co. and I got the distinct impression that he wasn't bothered if I went to Nantes or not.

I may have read the signs wrongly and he might be a really pleasant chap but we'll never know now.

Now, I didn't really do any touristy sightseeing while I was in Nantes and spent most of the limited daylight time around the offices talking to people. That was, after all, what I was there for and what I was getting paid for...

I honestly thought I'd be going back again - either to live there permanently - or, at least, as part of the transition teams that were being talked about to move all the office work and production over to Nantes during 1992.

So I thought I'd have plenty of opportunity to look around once the days were longer and the weather brighter.

I did the return journey to Peterborough – I'm sure it was on the Thursday – and in my confusion in the dark, I took the A3M out of Portsmouth instead of the M3 and it took me ages driving through the countryside to finally get to the M25. It was quite late by then so the rest of the route was straightforward.

By the time that I got back to Peterborough to weigh up my options, there had been some sort of change of heart in the German office and the option for me to go there had been withdrawn.

This was a bit of a blow as I had hoped to wangle a trip out to Germany to check out the Obertshausen operation – on the back of my Nantes trip - before making my final decision about where I wanted to go next. So it looked as if I would be going back to Nantes after all.

A few days later, I took some visitors from Nantes – Evelyne, I think, and somebody else - out for a visit to see a Baker Perkins G16 press running at Woodford in Witham, Essex. After that, I took them to nearby Stansted Airport so they could fly back to France and then I returned to our office in Peterborough, getting back quite late, around knocking off time.

During the time that we had been at Woodford, there had been a huge "about turn". Production was NOT going to be moved to Nantes after all – everything was going to Preston!

And I never travelled to France for work purposes again.

1995: French With Some Poles

The last time I had any specific involvement with French speaking customers was in April 1995 – and this was definitely a bit of an odd one.

By that time I was living in Preston and working from the RGS office there. The Peterborough Westfield Road factory had closed and all production had been moved to either Preston or the US. The Peterborough office staff had been greatly reduced and those that were left were in a much smaller rented office near Bretton Centre.

When I was still based in Peterborough, we used to have a monthly gathering called the Pre Contract Meeting which brought together representatives from all the various departments. The idea of this meeting was to flag up any orders that were in the pipeline but hadn't been announced yet and to highlight any issues that might crop up – rather than just waiting until they eventually did.

I had been the secretary for this meeting ever since it had started – much to the consternation of some of the old guard – so I produced the agenda and wrote up the minutes.

Once people from Preston became involved in contract and manufacturing matters, they started to attend the meetings as well – along with people from Allen Bradley Electronics in Milton Keynes, who were also part of the RGS group and took over the manufacture of the control systems after the closure of the former Bretton facility.

After a while, it made sense to rotate the venue for the meeting so that one month it was in Preston and the next in Peterborough. We also went down to Milton Keynes once and held the meeting at Allen Bradley.

For the first few meetings that we had in Preston, Anne came up to represent the Peterborough Commercial Department, which was nice, and holding meetings down in Peterborough as well gave me a good reason to pop back there from time to time.

Now, as I was in charge of this monthly meeting, I had the benefit of being able to decide when it would take place and I rather blatantly organised this to suit myself.

The meeting in Preston tended to take place on a Wednesday whereas the one we had at Milton Keynes was on a Friday – meaning that I could travel home on the Thursday evening, go to the meeting (Peterborough to Milton Keynes is only about 50 miles – Preston to Milton Keynes is 170...) and then stay in Peterborough for the weekend.

In the same way, Peterborough meetings often took place on a Thursday and I would try and find something really important that I needed to stay there for on the Friday to be able to make a weekend of it.

Now, it just so happens that I don't remember whether this particular instance that I am going to tell you about coincided with a Pre Contract Meeting or not. Whether it did or not, I was down in Peterborough a few days and there was a sales visit going on with some people from Poland.

Following the fall of communism and the opening up of the economies in eastern Europe in the early 1990s, there was a huge amount of activity in those areas and lots of people were trying to make deals of varying dubiousness.

One such chap was a middle man of some sort who wanted us to sell the repossessed G14 press from Sigma Prim - which had been in mothballs for several years – to a printing company in Poland who wanted to expand their business with new, more modern (to them...) equipment.

In order to keep the costs down, they wanted to buy it "as is", without any warranty or service back up, and were going to install it themselves. As this would still represent a huge investment for them as well as a big technical risk, they had come over to inspect the equipment, which was in storage at the now closed Westfield Road site.

I don't remember now how it came about that I was there for this but it must have been slightly more organised than I remember it being because I had a ticket for an all-ticket football match – Peterborough United away in Cambridge for the Saturday afternoon, which was 8th April.

My friend Graham Hill (he of cricket fame – who we have mentioned before...) lived in Cambridge at that time and he had arranged the tickets. Because the Cambridge ground only had a small capacity, it was always difficult to get tickets for that game and that was the only time I ever went there.

Anyway, I suppose it was because I was the only one who didn't have anything much else to do that I ended up chaperoning these Polish people while they were inspecting the press equipment in the store.

And boy - were they thorough! It wasn't just a quick look over. The mechanical guy checked the tightness of all the housings and the play in all the gears and the surface state of the cylinder bearers and the hose connections.... everything single little thing you could check, measure or adjust, he did. On everything...

I got bored stiff watching this after about 10 minutes but it just so happened that the press equipment was stored in the PMC fitting shop where I had used to work from 1985 to 1987 and it was also right in the area next to my old office. The office was still open but no longer used, so I was able to go in, sit down and reminisce.

The strange thing about this whole escapade – and the actual reason why it is included in my "France Actually" book, is that the head guy of the Polish group was fluent in French! Yes he was. Unusually for somebody growing up in an Eastern Bloc country, he had learnt French when he was young and was married to a French woman.

So, while the other guys were doing all their inspecting, we just nattered on in French the whole time - about the machine, about the factory, about my visits to Poland in 1990 and 1991, and about the world in general.

This was great for me because, by then, the linguistic content of my work in Preston had become very limited (read more about that in "Baker Perkins & Me" .... coming soon) and it had been several years since I had been able to have any sort of long in-depth conversations in French.

As far I can remember, they spent all day Thursday looking over the press equipment and all day Friday as well - and then the technical guy announced that he wanted to come back on Saturday morning and finish off!

This was a bit of a worry as I had planned to drive down to Cambridge in a relaxed manner and meet up with Graham and have something to eat and a pint or two before the game.

But work was work so I thought I'd better just hope for the best.

I went and ate with the Polish guys at their hotel – at their insistence - and they also gave me a very smart bottle of Polish vodka in a presentation box, which I quite possibly still have somewhere. We had a pleasant social evening - and didn't talk about work at all - and I was very relieved to hear that they, at least, wanted to make an early start the next day.

So, finally, around 12 noon on the Saturday morning, after another 3 hours or so and nattering in French with this pleasant and interesting Polish guy, the inspection was over and they got ready to drive all the way back home to Poland.

I drove straight down to Mr Hill's in Cambridge – it was only 40 miles and, despite being a bright sunny day with little traffic on the road, it seemed to take forever!

Having not had much breakfast before going into the factory, I was absolutely ravenous by now so we went and had a nibble before the game at a suitable hostelry which was pretty much on the way.

I recall this quite distinctly as we both opted for the all day breakfast and - just as we were in a hurry that day – it literally took "all day" to arrive!

Also - as far as I can remember, it is the only time in my life that I have ever eaten bacon, eggs, sausages, toast etc accompanied by a pint of lager shandy.

(Ever since I got my car licence, I have only drunk shandy when I have been out driving anywhere. I now hardly ever drink any alcohol at all and couldn't even tell you the last time I had a beer of any description...)

The very thought of that combination now makes me feel quite ill but it seemed like quite a good idea at the time - and was certainly the most efficient way of making up for lost time and getting caught up on breakfast and pre match drinks.

As a Post Script:

The "Mighty Posh" (as we often erroneously refer to them) lost 2-0 away at Cambridge and were relegated at the end of the season – and to the best of my knowledge , the Polish company never bought the second hand printing press...

Above left: The Eiffel Tower with an illuminated display counting down the days to the new millenium (ie the year 2000...). Above right: Lucy and Jill outside the Palais de Chaillot at Easter 1998.

The Pont Alexandre III seen from the Bateau Mouche trip on the River Seine. It was named after Tsar Alexander III, the Russian ruler during whose reign the Franco-Russian Alliance was ratified.

PB in the Place Kléber in Strasbourg in May 1998 (Photo by Lucy London).

Easter 1998: Paris

Over Easter 1998, we decided to take a short break to Paris. As we were living in Luxembourg at the time (more about that another time), it was just a matter of a reasonably short train ride – about 3 hours to do the 280km.

My friend from University Jill (more about her another time as well...) had come down from Lübeck to stay with us for a few days so we decided to go off and do something a bit different – and Lucy's son Jimmy was off school so the 4 of us went together.

Looking back at the 1998 calendar, Easter Sunday fell on 12th April and I know that I was in Luxembourg for my birthday so I am guessing that this must have been the week before, ie: commencing Monday 6th April.

It was a pleasant journey and we went through an area of France that I hadn't been to before, going past Verdun - of WW1 fame - and Reims - of Joan of Arc fame, before arriving at the Gare De L'Est in the late afternoon.

We had arranged to meet somebody's relative for a meal after we had arrived – and I won't say who they were or whose relative they were as the next bit of this story doesn't reflect very well on them, unfortunately.

It was a lovely warm and bright spring evening and we met up and had a nice meal and a nice chat with them and their boyfriend.

Afterwards, they took us to the hotel that they had reserved for us and we said our goodbyes as they had something else they needed to do - and we were quite tired by then after the journey. Safari, so goodie...

We checked into the hotel and were given the room keys and I got the feeling that the guy on reception looked a bit surprised to see us – despite the fact that the relative's boyfriend had clearly made the reservations for us.

As we went up to the rooms – two next door to each other – I got a sinking feeling and, when we saw the actual rooms, we saw why. It was very grotty and I began to wonder whether it might be "that sort of hotel...".

That's not to say that I had ever been in "that sort of hotel" before in order to be able to recognise one – but the whole place just had the sort of feel of one of those dubious establishments that they have in American crime dramas where hitmen and escaped convicts go to hide out in.

We had a hurried group discussion and were unanimous that we couldn't possibly stay there, so we grabbed our bags and went down to reception to say that we were leaving.

The shifty guy on reception was most put out and accused us of having "used the room" – whatever that was supposed to mean – particularly as we had an 11 year old boy with us... and this reinforced our belief that it was not the right sort place for us to be staying in. After all, if it was like that in daylight, what the hell would it be like after dark?

I don't really understand why the relative / boyfriend had booked us into such an unpleasant hotel. Living in the area, they must have known what was nice and what wasn't. I wondered afterwards if they had been worried that we had expected them to pay for it and that, being hard up, they had called in a favour....

Anyway, we extricated ourselves from that unpleasant place and wandered the streets of Paris trying to find somewhere nicer to stay. We didn't really know where we were going and it was dark by that time - so not much fun at all.

We headed back towards the station as there are usually plenty of hotels around railway stations and eventually found a nice bright clean looking place called the "Royal Dutch Hotel" – or something like that. I never managed to establish what was supposed to be "Royal" or "Dutch" about it, but at least there weren't hoards of prostitutes and drug dealers hanging around, so that was a good sign.

As well as being clean and pleasant, this hotel was horrendously expensive so we just booked in for the one night as a temporary measure and vowed to find somewhere more suitable in daylight.

Next morning after breakfast I borrowed the hotel copy of the "Pages Jaunes" and used the pay phone in the reception area to ring round and try and find somewhere cheaper to stay.

Don't forget that this was during the Easter Holidays so the whole world was there to enjoy "Paris in the Spring" and it meant that all of the cheaper tourist hotels were fully booked.

I eventually managed to find us a room at the Novotel Porte D'Orléans and, having stayed in Novotels before in France, knew that this would be a safe choice for us.

They were also very busy and only had one family room that we all had to squeeze into – but it was certainly better than going home early.   By the time that we had finally got there and got settled in, it was quite late so we decided to eat in the hotel and save our energies for the main sightseeing the next day.

However, just to make the most of the fact that we were in Paris, I took Jill on the Metro down to the banks of the Seine and we had a walk along where the booksellers have their stalls - and also got a great view of Notre Dame Cathedral in the evening twilight.

The next day – our main / only day for Paris sightseeing – it was absolutely chucking it down with rain. This was disappointing as the day before – that we had spent trying to find new accommodation - had been really nice – plus, as the weather had been generally mild, I didn't even have a coat with me.

Anyway, undaunted, we got the Metro into central Paris and headed for the Arc de Triomphe.

While we were there, we had a very funny experience in McDonald's and I wrote up a detailed account just after it happened.

And here it is:

Phoebe Cates And The McDonald's Milkshake Incident

It was a very wet and grey Tuesday morning on the Champs Elysees and after getting windswept and drenched looking around the base of the Arc de Triomphe, we were compelled by the youngest member of our group to take refuge in McDonalds for lunch.

It was extremely busy and we thought we would have trouble getting a seat but the upper level was being patrolled by some chic-looking ladies in turquoise coloured designer suits who were helping people to find suitable empty tables.

We ended up around to the left in a no smoking area and were happy to find a 4 seater table. As I took my seat, I noticed on the table next to us a couple of women with a couple of kids, obviously making the most of the Easter holidays to do some Parisien shopping and a bit of sightseeing.

My gaze hovered a little longer than usual on the lady to my left as I thought I recognised her. After a quick double take, I looked to see if any of my companions had noticed anything special and realising that they hadn`t, I then wondered how I might draw their attention to the interesting presence on the table next to us.

I picked up the McDonalds "Guide to Paris" map that I had taken from the distributor downstairs and then tried to find a pen in my pocket to write a note announcing what I had seen.

Not finding one, I snapped, `give me a pen quick..` in hushed tones, trying not to draw too much attention to what I was doing whilst at the same time, finding it hard to contain my excitement. After what seemed like an age, a pen was finally produced and I scribbled hurriedly on a blank space on the paper:

`Famous actress sitting behind Jimmy`

and then, just to make sure, added

`Phoebe Cates was in Lace....`

Jill took one look at the paper followed by a quick look over Jimmy`s shoulder and then hissed `Gremlins...?`. Having not seen `Gremlins`, I couldn`t comment although I had seen her in `Lace`, `Lace 2`, `Drop Dead Fred` (starring Rik Mayall) and most recently on TV over Christmas in `Princess Carabou`.

Lucy was the coolest of us all and gracefully stood up to `go to the toilet` just so that she could get a good look without making it too obvious.

By this time, from her glances towards us, it seemed obvious that Phoebe had realised that we had recognised her but she also seemed grateful that I hadn`t blurted it out and started bothering her for autographs and so on.

I was wracking my brains to try and remember which famous actor Phoebe Cates was married to. Then it dawned on me - Kevin Kline - of `Fish Called Wanda`, `French Kiss` and `In and Out` fame amongst many others. So, we were dining in the presence of beautiful Hollywood actress Phoebe Cates and also Kevin Kline`s offspring!

While Lucy was at the toilet, a milkshake went flying off the table and landed on the floor between Phoebe`s table and ours. Her two children - a boy and a girl - started squabbling over whose fault it had been and I spotted an excellent opportunity to involve myself in the discussion by grabbing Lucy's coat off her chair and furiously brushing it down as if to indicate that it had been splashed by the acrobatic beverage.

Within seconds, more McDonald's staff than you have ever seen in your life descended on the scene to mop up the puddle and, after I had used my French to explain what had been dropped on the floor, one of the chic ladies presented the group with a replacement drink.

During all this, the boy had decided that one of the pieces off his Kids Meal toy had gone flying off somewhere - a fact that had not escaped my notice.

So, whilst maintaining a general air of calm on the outside, I was also frantically scanning the surrounding floor with the corner of one eye to try and find it and heroically present it to his mother.

Eventually, the other lady - obviously Phoebe`s friend and confidante for such outings – our quite possibly a nanny of some sort - circled our table and found the missing item on the floor behind me somewhere.

It would seem that she had also been whipped up in the excitement of the moment as she announced to the boy – completely untruthfully, I might add - that the part must have `hit that man on the head....` at which point I started rubbing my forehead in mock agony and smiling at the kiddy, telling him how much it hurt.

His mother smiled at me again as if to show her appreciation for the way I was playing along with her son.

Then Lucy returned and, having made our meal last as long as we could possibly drag it out for, we decided it was time to leave. The Cates/Klines also prepared to leave at this point, with Phoebe putting the kids` coats on and her friend clearing the rubbish away.

What was quite amusing was that a quick glance around the upper floor showed that we had gained a whole audience of young damp French people staring in bedraggled and open mouthed amazement at what was going on before their eyes - so I decided to make the most of it by ensuring that we left at the same time as the Cates/Klines.

As we were about to go down the stairs, the boy came up to me, stuck his model in my stomach and said `bye` - a greeting that was accompanied by another sweet smile from Phoebe.

They had a chauffeur driven car parked on the Champs Elysees waiting for them and we continued on our walk down towards the Place de la Concorde in the wind and the rain. I was still floating from the experience and didn`t really come back down to earth until we reached FNAC.

273

Meanwhile, on the lower floor, unbeknown to me at the time, another French-farcical scenario had been unfolding. As she had emerged from the toilets, Lucy noticed a flurry of excitement among the chic, designer-clad ladies in the reception area.

One of their number had been designated to take the replacement milkshake up to the `petit garnement` whose flying drink had graced the upper floor. With much smirking , rolling of her eyes and a very slow, hip swaying walk (very definitely worthy of an Oscar), the lady concerned climbed the stairs directly in front of Lucy and wove her way gracefully between the crowded tables to present the by then unwanted drink with a magnificent flourish. Was that applause we heard...?

P.S. Lucy (call me Cassandra) remains unshakably convinced that the lovely Madame Kline was so completely and utterly bowled over by Paul`s dark good looks and his gallant, gentlemanly behaviour that she is now searching the streets of Paris for him so that she may ask him to star with her in her next film.   Watch this space!

PPS. Well, it is now 2021 and Phoebe Cates has never got in touch.... I wonder if she has written about the Paris McDonald's Milkshake Incident in her memoirs as well...?

*****

Right, back to the main narrative: After we had emerged from McDonalds, it was still raining – although not quite as heavily – but, rather than miss out on the whole of the day's sightseeing because your's truly didn't have a coat, we decided to bite the bullet and buy one.

There was an impressive looking menswear shop a few doors further along the Champs D'Elysee called Celio – which I had never heard of before or since - but they appear to have three outlets in chic areas of Paris these days, so must be pretty good.

We went in and I bought a heavy duty rain mac and a contrasting waterproof cap - and they are actually very good as I still have them now and have worn them often.

Anyway, this enabled us to brace against the weather and set off to get the Metro and go and see the Eiffel Tower.

We went to the Palais de Chaillot and the Trocadero Esplanade, which is by far the best place to see the Tower from. The rain had stopped although it was still rather overcast so we were able to stand and marvel at the views and take a few photos without getting soaked through.

Then we went down to the bank of the River Seine and decided to take a cruise round on the famous Bateaux Mouches – which I had never done before.

Lucy had lived in Paris for a while when she was younger and, therefore, knew about these things. She suggested that we would get to see more sights in one go on the boat trip – and it would be much less tiring than if we tried to walk round everywhere on foot and by metro.

So we did and it was nice to see all the ornate bridges as we went under them and many interesting buildings along both sides of the river viewed from a different angle to normal.

By the time we had got off the boat, the sun had come out and it was quite a nice afternoon. We decided to have a leisurely walk along the river bank and see where we ended up.

I don't actually remember where we ended up but it was a nice afternoon whatever we ended up doing. I think after a rather varied and exciting day, we headed back to the hotel and had a meal there before getting ready to travel back to Luxembourg the next day.

Rather ironically, the next day was bright and sunny. We got to the Gare De L'Est in plenty of time for the train back and were able to sit outside at a pavement cafe for a drink before embarking.

May 1998: Strasbourg

At the beginning of May 1998 we took another trip from Luxembourg back into France. This time we went to Strasbourg, where Lucy had lived and worked for time and still had some friends there.

Because of the location of European Institutions in both Luxembourg and Strasbourg, the two cities are well connected and there are plenty of trains throughout the day. It is around 160km and the journey time is between 2 and 3 hours depending on which service you take.

Upon arrival in Strasbourg, we got a taxi to the hotel that we had carefully selected and booked in advance – the Novotel (ta-dah!) – and, once we had settled in, Lucy's friend came and picked us up and took us back to theirs for the afternoon.

They had a nice long catch up chat and then we went for a walk with their dogs out along the river. After that we had a nice meal accompanied by some Cremant D'Alsace (look it up, it's very nice...) and were driven back to our hotel.

The next day we had a leisurely walk around the centre of Strasbourg, checking out some of Lucy's old haunts. At her suggestion, we also took a pleasure cruise along the River Rhein, which was useful as it had a commentary of the history of the city and pointed out all the main attractions, including the new European Parliament building which was still being completed

There was a cinema close to our hotel and in the evening we went to see the French comedy film "Dîner Des Cons" – which was remade in 2010 as an American comedy by Paramount Pictures called "Dinner For Schmucks".

We travelled back to Luxembourg on the train the next day – and that is the last time I ever set foot in France. I drove through the bit at the top near Calais a few times on the way to somewhere else but May 1998 is the last time that I visited anywhere in France and, with all the problems associated with travel in these modern times – terror attacks, virus pandemics and the like - I don't see that changing any time soon...

Travelling Across France But Not Actually Going There.

The Channel Tunnel opened in 1994 and I have travelled through it several times by car – using the Euroshuttle service - and once by train using the Eurostar.

Interestingly enough, while each of those journeys has taken me across French soil, not once have I ever actually set foot in France during them nor was I actually travelling to a French destination.

For the record – below is a list of occasions when I have travelled through France without actually going there. The journeys concerned will be explained in more depth in a later volume.

(Please note: the French end of the Channel Tunnel is actually at Coquelles but I have referred to "Calais" here as it is easier to remember.)

December 1997:	Drove home for Christmas from Luxembourg via Belgium and Calais. (1 way trip on Euroshuttle, drove to Luxembourg via Hoek van Holland / Germany beforehand and drove back to Luxembourg via Hoek van Holland and Germany again afterwards)
May 1998:	Drove to England from Luxembourg with Lucy to look at Universities. (2 way trip on Euroshuttle) 390Km Lux to Calais
June 1998:	Moved with Lucy from Luxembourg to England (1 way trip on Euroshuttle)
January 1999:	Drove my car back from Lucy's sister at Wittlich, Germany, through Belgium to Calais (400km) (1 way trip on Euroshuttle, flew to Frankfurt beforehand)
June 2000:	Drove to Luxembourg via Calais and Belgium to see Lucy's son's school graduation. (2 way trip on Euroshuttle)
February 2002:	Took Eurostar passenger service from Brussels to London (flew to Brussels beforehand).
March 2002:	Drove to Brussels via Calais (200km). Drove back (2 way trip on Euroshuttle)

NORTH / SOUTH DIVIDE
WHY NOT COLLECT THE SET?

North / South Divide: The Original

The 2013/14 season was a watershed year for me ice hockey wise. The Fylde Flyers team finished, leaving me with only recreational hockey to write about in Blackpool so I decided to branch out and cover the English National League in a more general manner.

What you will find in this book is a mixture of opinion columns written for Blueliner.com and round-ups and news items that started off on bestkeptsecrets and, after January 2014, ended up on icehockeyreview.co.uk. I hope that makes sense – it shouldn't be boring, anyway...!

ISBN: 9798563183759

Volume 2: Ice Hockey And Me

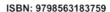

Mainly autobiographical and featuring random and bizarre topics such as:

How I came to be at the World Championships in Luxembourg,
The day I met Stewart Roberts,
Which Sims twin is which and
The story behind Lucy's "French And Ormes" poem...

ISBN: 9781909643451

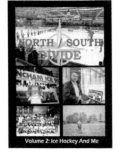

Volume 3: Cricket & Baseball

More autobiography - mainly about my involvement in cricket and baseball – plus a few other things as well.

So, just to whet your appetite, in this volume you can read all about:
Why I wasn't any good at cricket at school
The Cricket World Cup in 1999
The Preston Bobcats league baseball team
The Preston University student team of 1996/97
And my experiences of baseball coaching at Summer Camps in the Czech Republic.

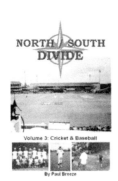

ISBN: 9781909643468

The

North / South Divide: Volume 5
By Paul Breeze

Volume 5: The Bachelor Pad Years

Nope – not a "tell-all" exposé, but a bit more autobiography based mostly around the period 1989 to 1993.

Featuring such varied and bizarre topics as:
- Being young in England in the 1980s and 90s
- All the fun of the two Bachelor Pads in Peterborough and Preston
- The trials and tribulations of girls, girl friends and girlfriends
- Visits to countries that don't exist any more such as Czechoslovakia, Yugoslavia and East Germany.
- Football, music, ice hockey, cars - and all that jazz!

ISBN: 9781909643482

North / South Divide - Volume 5
by Paul Breeze

COMING SOON

Volume 6: Germany Calling

Yes - this volume is about trips to Germany plus other places in that general direction, including Belgium, Luxembourg, Czech Republic and Austria.

There's a bit of work related content including the DRUPA exhibitions in Düsseldorf in 1990 and 1995 and the year I spent in Luxembourg working for a radio station and a media agency.

So, if you are interested in travel trivia, this book may well be for you – when it comes out, anyway...

All books listed on these pages are available now by mail order from Amazon, Posh Up North, Waterstones, Book Depository and all other quality outlets.

ICE HOCKEY BOOKS BY PAUL BREEZE

Ice Hockey (1936) by Major BM Patton - Annotated & Illustrated 2020: A facsimile reprint of the original 1936 edition with new introduction, author biography and appendices.

ED2n 11/12: A Review of the 2011/12 Ice Hockey Season In English Division 2 North

Ice Hockey Review 12/13 North: A Review of the 2012/13 Ice Hockey Season in NIHL North Divisions 1 & 2

Ice Hockey Review NIHL Yearbook 2014: The 2013/14 Season in NIHL N&S Divisions 1 & 2

Ice Hockey Review NIHL Yearbook 2015: The 2014/15 Season In NIHL North & South

Ice Hockey Review NIHL Yearbook 2016

Ice Hockey Review UK Hockey Yearbook 2017

Ice Hockey Review UK Hockey Yearbook 2018

Fylde Flyers - A Complete Record: Seasons 2011/12 & 2012/13

The Seagull Has Landed: A Light-Hearted Review Of the First 12 Months Back Together Of the Blackpool Seagulls Ice Hockey Team

A Year In The Wild: The 2016/17 season following Widnes Wild

Widnes Wild – Lockdown Lookback

North / South Divide: Random Ramblings About British Ice Hockey During the 2013/14 Season

I have also made contributions to:

The History Of Ice Hockey In Peterborough by Stuart Latham

60 Years Of The Altrincham Aces by Stuart Latham

The Deeside Dragons by Stuart Latham

From Vikings To Devils by Stuart Latham

Wightlink Raiders – Simply The Best by Chris Randall

UK Ice Hockey by Michael A Chambers

And I also produced commemorative match programmes for:

Blackpool Seagulls v UK Firefighters Charity Game (February 2012)

Blackpool Seagulls Bruce Sims Visit (April 2013)

Deeside Dragons v Liverpool Leopards Legends Match (July 2013)

Bob Kenyon Memorial Shield Game (June 2016)

I also provided weekly league round up columns for the Blackburn Hawks Match programmes for 3 seasons and series of "Rewind" nostalgia articles for 1 season.

Also numerous contributions to various play off and cup end of season programmes.

In addition, Paul Breeze had co-written, edited, or helped to publish all of the following:

Nov 2000: The History of Rot Weiss Erfurt: Forgotten Champions of DDR Football (Edition out of print)

Dec 2001: Darwen Football Club: Memories

Dec 2002: Colne Giants: Tales from the Forgotten World of Knur and Spell

Mar 2007: Blackpool to Bond Street!: The Fascinating Story of Amy Blackburn - Pioneer of the Makeover

May 2012: Guns & Pencils: An Anthology Of War Poems

Sep 2012: Twilight: A Single Act Stage Drama Written with Mature Actors in Mind...

Oct 2012: Bullets & Daffodils: The Wilfred Owen Story (Edition out of print)

Oct 2012: Selected Poems: Over 50 of the Best Entries for the 2012 Pendle War Poetry Competition

Oct 2012: A Tale Of Two Sisters: An Original Screenplay Suitable For TV or Film

Jan 2013: ED2n 11/12: A Review of the 2011/12 Ice Hockey Season in English Division 2 North

Feb 2013: Purple Patches: A Collection of Poems, Songs and Short Stories from the Fountain Pen of Lucy London

Apr 2013: The Seagull Has Landed!: A Light Hearted Review of the First 12 Months Back Together of the Blackpool Seagulls Ice Hockey Team

Jul 2013: Female Poets of the First World War: Part of an Ongoing International Centenary Research Project: Volume 1

Sep 2013: Ice Hockey Review 12/13 North: A Review of the 2012/13 Ice Hockey Season in NIHL North Divisions 1 & 2

Nov 2013: Pendle War Poetry Competition - Selected Poems: An Anthology of Over 100 of the Best Poems Submitted for the 2013 Pendle War Poetry Competition: 2013

Sep 2014: No Woman's Land: A Centenary Tribute to Inspirational Women of World War One

Oct 2014: Ice Hockey Review - NIHL Yearbook 2014: The 2013/14 Season in NIHL North & South

Nov 2014: Hearts in Unison: A New Collection of Poems by Natasha Walker

Nov 2014: Respect The 88: A collection of verse about - or inspired by - the Ingleborough Road Memorial Playing Field

Aug 2015: Love & War - 2015 Reprint: A Collection of Poems by "Nadja" - Later Marchesa Nadja Malacrida - Originally Published in 1915

Oct 2015: Ice Hockey Review NIHL Yearbook 2015 Sponsored by Red Hockey: The 2014/15 Season in NIHL North & South

Dec 2015: Faith Finds Out: A Short Story About The First World War (Kindle only - short story)

Dec 2015: Magical Mystery Christmas (Kindle only - short story)

Apr 2016: Fylde Flyers - A Complete Record: Seasons 2011/12 & 2012/13

Apr 2016: Women Casualties of the Great War in Military Cemeteries: (In Support of) Wenches in Trenches - Roses of No Man's Land: Volume 1: Belgium & France – limited charity edition

Jun 2016: The Somme - 1916: A Centenary Collection of Poets, Writers & Artists Involved in the 1916 Offensive

Sep 2016: Female Poets of the First World War: Volume 2

Sep 2016: Women Casualties of the Great War in Military Cemeteries: Volume 1: Belgium & France

Oct 2016: Ice Hockey Review NIHL Yearbook 2016

Jun 2017: A Year In the Wild: The 2016/17 season following Widnes Wild in the NIHL North Laidler Conference

Oct 2017: Ice Hockey Review UK Hockey Yearbook 2017

Apr 2018: Arras, Messines, Passchendaele And More: Poets, Writers, Artists & Nurses in 1917

Jul 2018: Aviator Poets & Writers Of WW1: with a special section on women pilots

Aug 2018: Poets' Corners In Foreign Fields: A Guide to Literary Graves in Military Cemeteries

Oct 2018: Ice Hockey Review UK Hockey Yearbook 2018

Oct 2018: Pendle War Poetry - Selected Poems 2018: Under 18 & Overseas Entries

Oct 2018: Pendle War Poetry Competition - Selected Poems 2018: United Kingdon & Ireland Entries

Oct 2018: Post 1945 German Cinema - Two DEFA Films: Comparing "Die Legende von Paul und Paula" & "Solo Sunny"

Oct 2018: Francois Mitterrand & Margaret Thatcher: A Comparison Of Leadership Styles

Oct 2018: The BBC And Radio Luxembourg: A Comparison Of Broadcasting Styles and Attitudes

Nov 2018: Merseyside Poets, Writers & Artists Of The First World War

Jan 2019: White Feather: An original song by Lucy London - arranged for a 7-Piece Band.

Jun 2019: Great War Memorial Birthday Book: Birthdates of Poets, Writers, Artists & Nurses From the First World War With Space To Keep A Note Of Your Own Memorable Dates

Nov 2019: The Adventures Of Bunny, Archie, Alice & Friends

Feb 2020: Wilfred Owen: Centenary: Featuring Brief Owen Biography, Wilfred Owen And Me, Wilfred Owen In Print & Birkenhead Centenary Commemorations.

Oct 2020: Ice Hockey (1936) by Major BM Patton - Annotated & Illustrated 2020: A facsimile reprint of the original 1936 edition with new introduction, author biography and appendices

Nov 2020: Nadja - The Complete Poems

Nov 2020: Widnes Wild - Lockdown Lookback

Nov 2020: North / South Divide: Random Ramblings About British Ice Hockey During THE 2013/14 Season

Dec 2020: Artists Of The First World War: Volume 1

May 2021: The Lucy London Songbook

Aug 2021: Wightlink Raiders - Simply The Best: The 25 Year History of Ice Hockey on the Isle Of Wight

Sep 2021: North / South Divide – Volume 2: Ice Hockey And Me

Nov 2021: North / South Divide Volume 3: Cricket & Baseball

Copies of most publications are available via Amazon, PoshUpNorth.com, Waterstones, Book Depositary and many other quality outlets. Certain titles are available as Kindle download.

INTERESTING WEBSITES

If you have found any of this in the least bit interesting, you might like to have the occasional look at some of these various websites which, as of March 2022, I am currently involved with:

Check out our audio and video archive in our dedicated "Paul & Lucy's Best Kept Secrets" YouTube channel at www.youtube.com.

IF YOU HAVE ENJOYED THIS BOOK, YOU WILL ABSOLUTELY <u>LOVE</u>
"The Bachelor Pad Years"

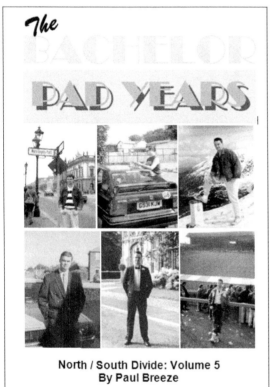

North / South Divide: Volume 5
By Paul Breeze

ISBN-13: 978-1-909643-48-2

Full Contents List:
Preamble: Girls At School, Girl Friends and Girlfriends
1984: Literally!
September 1989: Amsterdam
1990: Welcome To The Bachelor Pad
Spring 1990: Caribbean Interlude
April 1990: Drupa Exhibition
May 1990: Berlin
May 1990: Amsterdam 2
Belinda Carlisle / Erasure/ The Stranglers & Other Musical Memories
August 1990: Paul Gets A Car
September 1990: Polish Pursuits 1 – Trip To Zakopane
Autumn 1990: Nordic No Go
April / May 1991: Polish Pursuits 2 - Visit To Warsaw
1991: A Little Bit Of Lynda
Autumn 1991: Whitney Houston & Roxette
September 1991: Inter Rail
December 1991: Chris Rea / Spain
Squash 1985-1995
Football In The Bachelor Pad Years
Ice Hockey In The Bachelor Pad Years
1992-93: The Bachelor Pad Mk2, Preston
1992 & 93: Jola In England

Available March 2022 by Mail Order from Amazon, Posh Up North, Waterstones, Book Depository and all other quality outlets.

Printed in Great Britain
by Amazon